Guide to the wines of
Germany

HANS SIEGEL

Series Editor
PAMELA VANDYKE PRICE

With illustrations by
VANA HAGGERTY

GH00694940

PITMAN

To three great lovers of German Wines:
my father, my friend and partner Ian Peebles,
and my wife Betty.

PITMAN PUBLISHING LIMITED
39 Parker Street, London WC2B 5PB

Associated Companies
Copp Clark Ltd, Toronto
Fearon-Pitman Publishers Inc, Belmont, California
Pitman Publishing Co. SA (Pty) Ltd, Johannesburg
Pitman Publishing New Zealand Ltd, Wellington
Pitman Publishing Pty Ltd, Melbourne

Text set in 10/11 pt Baskerville by Carlinpoint Ltd.,
Printed in Great Britain by Billing & Sons Limited,
Guildford, London and Worcester

ISBN 0 273 01096 4

Contents

Foreword

A guide to the wines of Germany should, like all guides, be informative, authoritative and gentle. It must not frighten the reader with technicalities or bore him with abstruse professional disputes. It should present a true objective picture, deepen the reader's interest in German wines and sharpen his desire for more information.

Of the many books on German wines some are oenological or viticultural, some geographical and chemical, and others touristic or just autobiographical. Recent publications show a very high technical standard, though those from semi-official German sources, perhaps understandably, sometimes look at their subject through rose-tinted spectacles. Frequently there is too much emphasis on Wine Law and particularly the Law of 1971. There have been Wine Laws in the past and there will be in the future, if only to define and classify in the light of progress; good wine is entirely due to the winemaker's art.

In my guide, supported by the stimulating influence of my editor, I have aimed to show how wine, a pleasure to mankind since Noah, has in Germany achieved a type and excellence of its own. Germany produces a mass of highly drinkable wines, many very good and memorable ones, and quite a few of really great excitement and joy to the senses and intellect.

I would like to offer my thanks to those who have helped in the preparation of this book, especially to Pamela Vandyke Price, who put in far more work than her editorial role would justify, to the German Food Centre, and, last but not least, to the Wines from Germany Information Service, at whose birth I assisted, and who were most generous in their help with illustrations and statistics.

There is no mystery about tasting and enjoying wine. Everybody is born with a pair of ears, two eyes and a palate, and just as it is up to the individual to decide on his preference between the Beatles or Beethoven, the 'Blue Period' of Picasso or Rembrandt's self-portraits, so there can be as much fun in developing one's palate by tasting these fascinating wines from Germany and making friends with them. I hope this guide will help.

The German Vineyards

German vineyards are the most northerly in the world, excepting those of England. They are situated between the latitudes 48° and 50°, on the same level as Vancouver and Winnipeg. German wine production is small and cannot alone satisfy the demand of the German populace; at 10,000,000 hectolitres a year, production is well below that of France, Italy, Spain, Portugal, the Soviet Union and even the United States.

Germany exports 700,000 hectolitres of wine a year but it also imports 7,000,000 hectolitres, largely of inexpensive red and white wines. These are astonishing figures, which might seem to minimise the importance of German wines on export markets, but there is no respectable restaurant, hotel or wine merchant anywhere in the world who does not, as a matter of course, stock three or four German wines, bearing classic names. There are many other outlets which will offer a very much wider range. How is this contradiction explained? Why has this tiny production achieved and maintained its influence and importance all over the world of wine?

What is unique about German wines?

They show the fundamental superiority of a fruit matured in a temperate climate, just as an English (or German) garden peach tastes much better than one from Spain or Italy. You can smell and taste the floweriness of the grape, which is not possible in the wines of those countries where the vineyards endure a burning hot southern sun.

Then, the particular layering and character of the soil in Germany allows the vine to absorb ideal nourishment without effort. Above all, the carrier of all taste and the backbone of longevity is natural fruit acidity; in temperate climates such as that of Germany this is fully maintained and acts as a base for the development of the myriads of higher alcohols, esters, aldehydes and all the other aromatic particles which form the whole sensory perception. Add to these ideal conditions for fine wine production the art and skill of the grower in selecting the right grape and looking after it and also that of the wine maker, who supervises the processes of vinification and of maturation with all the resources of science.

It is this set of circumstances, plus the man-made skills, that enable the grape to display its style — indeed, its stylishness. Style makes the man, it is said; certainly it is style that makes fine wine. The grape that grows in the classic wine regions of Germany can develop without any coarseness resulting from earthiness, or other factors detracting from its quality. It is because of this that German wines, at all price levels, have become famous and remained so throughout the world. There are no other wines like them — and there are no other vineyards like those of Germany either.

Climate

In general, the vineyards enjoy what is often called a 'continental' climate — warm summers and cold winters. They do, however, have this climate somewhat moderated, so that there are not the extremes of temperature experienced in countries further east, such as Poland. Humidity tends to be low, which is why the proximity of water in the rivers is helpful to the vineyards. Sunshine hours and rainfall vary from year to year, but hot, dry summers do occur, although not usually more than once in five years. The vine is a tough plant, it survives many climatic changes and has very deep roots to seek nourishment for the grapes, but it requires 100 days of sun from the date of its flowering in the spring to achieve complete maturity by the time of the vintage.

Vintages

Quality-wise it is possible to generalise and say that two years out of three will achieve 'six points out of ten', using wine trade marking terms. One year in five will reach eight points and one in ten will be perfect. There are, however, exceptions. 1945, 1947, 1949 and 1953 were all excellent years. The next great year was 1959, with good vintages in 1964 and 1967 too. 1971, the next best year after 1959, was excellent, 1972 and 1973 were, overall, only acceptable and 1974 wines tend to be somewhat short as regards taste. 1975 is most promising but seems unlikely to reach the perfection of 1971. 1976 was a very ripe, forthcoming year which produced very great wines, although some of the smaller grades may not be too long-lasting. 1977 is a pleasant if not outstanding vintage.

There has not been a really bad year for a long time, though temperature and weather vary in every district and make generalisations difficult. An exception was 1956, which produced a severe frost early in the winter and destroyed many vines; little wine of any quality could be made then. But even in the most adverse weather conditions, modern vinification and cellar methods now enable the wine maker to produce at least a passable wine, generally pleasant to drink. In such years he has breathing space in which to hope for a better vintage in the future and to be able to keep it to mature when nature is kind.

Where the vineyards are

To an observer on a satellite, the Rhine's river system must look like the elongated fuselage of an aircraft, with three wings tucked on each side and an S-bend in the middle. The first wing on the right (eastern) side is the River Neckar, the second wing is the River Main at the beginning of the S-bend. The third wing, the River Lahn, is almost opposite the left (western) wing, which is the Mosel. The north-western wing is the River Ahr, and the southern wing the Nahe, which is tucked in at the end of the S-bend.

Zell on the Mosel

The Rhine flows north from Basel in Switzerland for 180 miles until it reaches Mainz, where it turns west for twenty miles, then it runs north again through the Rhine Gorge. The stretch between Basel and Mainz is part of a low plain, which is twenty to fifty miles wide and is bordered by the Vosges and

Haardt Mountains on the west, with the Black Forest and the Odenwald to the east, and the Taunus and Hunsrück hills blocking the north and west. In pre-historic times the melting snow from the Alps drained into this plain and formed an enormous sea or lake, until, in the course of time, the waters found a weakness at the north-western side and slowly seeped through the hills at the narrows of Bingen and Rüdesheim.

Geologically, virtually every type of soil and sub-soil may be found in the German vineyards, from heavy clay to pure sand (this is noticeable near Mainz, where the most delicious asparagus is grown as well as the vine). It is this huge gamut of soil varieties that, to a large extent, accounts for the enormous variations in the character of German wines: they are the children of their homeland and vary just as it does.

German Wines in History

It is one of the wonders of wine that, in such a northern region as Germany, the vineyards began to be cultivated in comparatively early times. It is possible that the vine was brought from the Mediterranean to what were to become the German vineyard regions even before the arrival of the Roman legions, but there is not much documentation about this. Julius Caesar extended the frontiers of the Roman Empire to the left bank of the Rhine in 57-55 BC and then, of course, the army had to have its regular wine ration. It should not be forgotten that, in early times, this was almost as important as their bread: wine was the only beverage and, in areas where the water supply might be suspect, it served as a disinfectant. Wine acted as a tonic, a remedy, was used by doctors and surgeons (as an anaesthetic) and was far more essential to the maintenance of health than most people now realise; it was also, in northern countries, at least a means of getting some supply of vitamins during the winter, when vegetables and fruit would be difficult to find. And the Mediterranean soldier needed his wine ration to keep him warm and cheerful, in fighting trim, during the building of the great Roman Empire.

So it is very likely that wine supplies were sent up to Germany from this period, but it does not seem as if vines were planted there in substantial quantities until at least the beginning of the Christian era, when the Emperor Augustus' forces established the fortified town of Trier; from the second century onwards, vines were increasingly planted. The poets, both Ausonius in the third century, who wrote in detail about the Mosel, and Venantius Fortunatus, in the sixth century, who noted how the vineyards had spread enormously, with the vines climbing high, record the popularity of native-grown wine. Visitors to museums will find plenty of relics to interest them, the most famous probably being the 'wine ship' relief, showing casks being transported on the Mosel, which is in the Landesmuseum in Trier.

In spite of the appalling hardships suffered after the decline of the Roman Empire and during the various barbarian invasions and civil struggles, the cultivation of the vineyards continued. In the dark ages, it was the religious establishments, acting as schools, hospitals, pharmacies, hotels and market gardens, who maintained many vineyards, dominated by what were often very large establishments; the heads of these, bishops and archbishops, were like kings in their own territories.

With the beginning of the Holy Roman Empire, the vineyards received more encouragement, notably from Charlemagne, who, in the latter part of the eighth century, displayed great interest in vineyards in Germany as well as in France. The story is told how, when staying in his 'Pfalz' (fortress) at Ingelheim, the winter snows melted on these south-facing slopes more quickly than anywhere else; this was something that prompted him to suggest that this otherwise barren land might be profitably put under vines. Even after Charlemagne's death, folk tales were told of how the great Emperor would leave his tomb and wander through the vineyards by night, bestowing a benediction on them.

After this, the German vineyards were in the hands of the great landowners and smaller proprietors, as well as the religious houses. It should be remembered that Germany under the Holy Roman Empire consisted of numerous small states, each with its ruler. Rather surprisingly, however, German wines began to be exported at quite an early date, largely thanks to the circumstances of the rivers on whose banks many of the vineyards were sited; the wine was transported to the coastal ports and, from there, formed an important article of commerce in trade throughout northern Europe, including England. The great trading and banking houses that were growing up took full advantage of this trading boom and, in spite of wars and civil disturbances, German wines became known in markets far distant from their homeland. The Low Countries and Scandinavia were all buyers. Centres such as Trier, Mainz, Worms, Speyer, Würzburg and Heilbronn furthered the interest in German wine; these were places frequented by scholars, diplomats, the nobility (who often took holidays in the various spas) as well as the prosperous merchants, and all foreign visitors would gain some knowledge of the local wines, which they might take away with them. Nor should the significance of the great Jewish dynasties be forgotten — as businessmen, they too travelled far afield and they had always included the use of wine in their religious observances.

The Thirty Years' War was a terrible setback to wine cultivation and trade in general, but the great noble and religious holdings were maintained until, when Napoleon I began to extend his empire, he secularised the vineyards in 1803; some of the great estates of the nobility remained intact, but this was the beginning of the main change in the pattern of German wine production.

With the restoration of comparative tranquillity in Europe after the Battle of Waterloo in 1815, trade revived and businessmen began to act as intermediaries between growers and customers. These early wine merchants, based at first in the regions of wine production, progressively extended their operations; members of a wine family might be sent further afield, some of them overseas. It is from this time that some of the important German wine dynasties still in business today date their rise in prosperity; improved communications made it possible for wine in cask to be transported even across the Atlantic and arrive in drinkable condition. German wines became known to a wider public, and when the far-seeing Jewish wine families began to establish themselves in export markets, they developed their marketing of the wines that they had known and loved. Many chose to uproot themselves, in the wave of emigration to America in the nineteenth century, and some firms even moved their headquarters from Germany to US trading centres. With the high proportion of first-generation Americans who had left Germany in the Bismarck era, on account of wars and civil problems, there was a ready-made transatlantic market for these beloved wines prior to World War I.

Prohibition, introduced by Congress at the end of World War I, was naturally a blow to all wine-drinking in the US, but elsewhere the popularity of German wines spread; in Britain, of course, it had been much encouraged by the Royal Family's known liking for the wines. Queen Victoria, who had a German mother and married a German, visited Hochheim in 1850 and agreed to the site she saw being named after her: the Königin Viktoria-Berg.

In the 1870s the aphis, phylloxera vastatrix, which was destroying the rootstocks of all the European vineyards, also attacked those of Germany. Grafting on to resistant American rootstocks was undertaken in time to prevent the total destruction of the vineyards and all German wines are grafted today. The pest came to Europe from the US, so it seems fair that the New World also supplied the remedy.

The period between the two World Wars was a very anxious time for the German wine trade and quite disastrous for the Jewish merchants. With the return of peace, the rehabilitation of the vineyards and revival of trade had to be undertaken. Here, there is a remarkable thing to relate: in marketing wine, there has been no inflation, and the cost of a litre of wine filled today at the producer's cellar in Germany is exactly the same as it was a quarter of a century ago! The reason for this triumphant rebuttal of the idea that inflation is some kind of act of God is simple: output per unit of acreage has gone up dramatically, while labour costs have been heavily reduced, through the adoption of modern methods. As a stable commodity price is the basis of successful marketing, it is no wonder that the sales and popularity of German wines have gone on rising in the past twenty-five years.

In addition, of course, enormous progress has been made as regards vinification and bottling. In the era of the great estates, there were only a few vintners' co-operatives; nowadays, there are some regions where these co-operatives deal with the vast majority of the production. The very first co-operative was founded in the Ahr as early as 1868, by two men who were trying to help small growers; they founded these 'Weingärtner-genossenschaften' (wine-grower co-operatives, as they are called in Württemberg), thereby uniting those growers who had only small patches to cultivate and could not afford up-to-date equipment for making their wines correctly and caring for them once made. The improvement in quality was steady and today over 65,000 growers belong to around 400 co-operatives. 230 of these are reasonably large, with the remainder, of somewhat smaller size, acting in practice as subsidiaries of the bigger establishments. Over three-quarters of all co-op wines today are sold in bottles, and these wines receive skilled attention all through their processing. The co-operatives have

A modern wine cellar: Breisach, Baden

established large 'Zentralkellerei' which have taken over the vinification and handling of wine for some of the smaller nearby co-ops, in a number of regions. These are situated in Breisach (Baden), Mögglingen (Württemberg), Bernkastel (Mosel), Gau-Bickelheim (Rheinhessen), Bad Kreuznach (for the Nahe), and Repperndorf (Franconia). These central cellars are most impressive to visit, with batteries of giant tanks in stainless steel or plastic — each tank holding up to 50,000 gallons — and the most up-to-date bottling lines, laboratories and storehouses. It is from such installations that large distributors — wholesalers, supermarkets, and chain stores — are supplied; their wines may not be as exciting in quality as those produced in the cellars of the more specialised growers, but this ready availability of such a vast quantity of good sound wine has helped the industry enormously.

A number of old-established but small growers continue in existence, alongside the co-operatives; such growers can appraise each of their casks separately and each cask will possess its own style. Wines coming from the vast co-ops cannot have this sort of individuality and character, but it is their wines that satisfy the demands of the mass markets.

Another rather new method of marketing originated between the two World Wars. A Rheinhessen firm had the idea of sending out travellers to effect house-to-house sales by means of personal calls. Although a somewhat expensive method, this proved highly successful in the locality and, after World War II, the method was extended throughout Germany. Eventually, similar campaigns were launched in Britain and other export markets. They too have met with much success and the Pieroth establishment in particular exerts great influence in many wine producing regions.

The most important date in the recent history of German wines is probably 1971, when a new German Wine Law was introduced. This is not easy for the layman to understand — indeed, many growers have difficulty with it! Its complexities are briefly explained elsewhere (pages 42-8), but it is subject to constant review and revision. The most significant thing, as far as the ordinary wine drinker is concerned, is that the German Wine Law attempts to unify all the wines made in Germany, so that their labels give the potential customer consistent information as to exactly what the bottle contains and where it comes from. It should simplify many of the apparent difficulties that, in the past, have perplexed and deterred wine lovers outside Germany from getting to know more about these varied and beautiful wines.

How the Wines are Made

A grape on the vine is very small, vulnerable and perishable. Wine in the bottle lives for years and is impervious to outside influence apart from physical extremes. How does this metamorphosis come about? What is a vine, how does the vintner look after it and what process enables him to turn it into wine?

The Vines

The vine will grow almost anywhere, provided the soil is deep enough for its root system and the climate is not too wet. In Germany it thrives even on the steep stony slopes and terraces of the Mosel and Ahr where nothing else would, and feels as much at home on the undulating expanse of the Rheinhessen as on the gentle hills of Rheingau and Haardt.

Most Germany vines are now grafted on American root stock as protection against the aphis, phylloxera vastatrix. This tiny insect launched its first big attack on Europe from the U.S. during the 19th century and nearly succeeded in wiping out all the vineyards. At first producers were helpless, as the usual methods of spraying such insecticides as they had and disinfecting the soil did not work. The insect does its damaging work during the summer on leaves and branches but recedes to the roots during the winter and its life cycle is such that it can only be eradicated by flooding the vineyards, and keeping them so! It was found, just in time, that the roots of native American vines are resistant to phylloxera and, with its life cycle broken, the insect cannot survive. Recently there have been moves to return to planting the direct roots of the classic vinestocks, but unless different chemicals are found to fight the phylloxera scourge it is unlikely that the present method of grafting on American root stock will be given up, for, once in the soil, the aphis remains there. There have been arguments as to whether this root grafting has a detrimental influence on the quality of the grape and, eventually, the wine but it is difficult to arrange scientific comparisons, so it is now agreed that this problem can be disregarded.

Most vines begin life as cuttings in the nursery, where they are grafted on rootstock. Then, after a year or two, they are planted in the vineyard in rows sufficiently wide apart to allow mechanical cultivation (where this can be used) and are either trained along wires or up poles, depending on the local conditions and traditional methods of cultivation. The vine must be trained so that it is adequately exposed to the sun, not so near the ground as to be exposed to cold and wet, and able to take advantage of any protection afforded by the angle of the vineyard.

After four to six years the vineyard is ready to produce its first commercial crop; of course, grapes will have grown earlier; full productivity will be reached in ten to fifteen years. Though the vine will live to a great age, its productivity begins to decline slowly after about fifty years when it will be necessary to replant and replace the vines. Throughout its life, the behaviour of each vine will be recorded by markers and the types of vines are graded according to their output. This grading or 'klone selection' — selection of specific strains — has contributed enormously to the present high state of efficiency and output, both as regards quality and quantity. The German wine institutes are world famous for their work on grape varieties, the Institut für Rebenzüchtung und Rebenveredlung der Forschungsanstalt (Institute for Vine Breeding and Grafting) at Geisenheim being perhaps the most important.

The Grapes

The choice of grape is one of the decisive factors of viticulture. Grapes vary so much that they can almost change their basic character as the result of being planted in different places; the right grape must be chosen for each particular area. With the exception of the Elbling, most of today's great traditional grape species are, historically speaking, comparatively young and their line of development has not been recorded for more than a few hundred years. One might have assumed that the great religious houses, keepers of literature and nurseries of science during the Middle Ages, would have observed and recorded many details of viticulture with keen interest and that they would have been able to make suggestions as to improvements, but only very little written evidence is available about this.

The greatest and most famous grape variety in Germany is the **Riesling** — the first syllable of Riesling, by the way, is pronounced to rhyme with 'geese'. Not very impressive to look at, it has smallish, green-yellow berries, and its almost undersized leaves turn yellow rather early in the year. But the Riesling, like most of the old traditional vines originating in south-east Europe, is a hardy plant, almost impervious to early and late frost and staunch on most types of soil, from rich loam to slate on rock-like precipitous terraces. It matures late and, given the right weather conditions, produces wines of unsurpassable quality. They excel by their great bouquet, fruit and body; they are virile and strong, with outstanding all-round harmony and they have enormous staying power, especially among white wines, which do not usually have the long lives of certain reds.

The Riesling is, of course, famous all over the world. But the true German Riesling must not in any way be confused with other varieties, nor with grapes which, because their names give the impression that they are some type of Riesling, make wines of totally different style.

Within Germany itself, the Riesling can vary enormously but, as the White Riesling, it seems, according to Professor Doctor Helmut Becker, of the Vine Institute at Geisenheim, to have had its origins in the wild vines that still grow in the Rhine Valley. Today, it is generally referred to simply as 'Riesling' and not White Riesling, but there is a local name for it even within Germany — Klingelberger, in Baden; this version of the name probably comes from the Klingelberg vineyard, near the Castle of Staufenberg in Durbach, where the Riesling was first planted in 1797.

In the past, buyers of vinestocks would purchase these according to their origin, thus the descriptions 'Rheinriesling' and 'Moselriesling' were used, although it has only been in recent times that scientific knowledge has enabled it to be established that one vine from a particular area truly is the same type as one from somewhere else. But from these geographical names, the terms 'Rheinriesling' and 'Johannisberger' or 'Johannisberger Riesling' came into use, the former term being common in south and south-western Europe, the latter being used in America.

Most confusingly, many countries term certain of their wines 'Riesling' when they are made from the Welsch Riesling, a very different species from the Rhine Riesling. In the USA, for example, the word 'Riesling' can be prefaced by the following terms — Grey, Emerald, Missouri, Franken; in Canada there is an Okanegan Riesling, in Australia there are 'Rieslings' from the Hunter Valley and Clare, and an SA or South African Riesling appears in South Africa. But wines made from these grapes are not to be confused in any way with those made from the true White Riesling, the Riesling of Germany. Professor Becker is firm that in Germany itself, the Welsch Riesling is not planted in any vineyard.

In Switzerland the cross of the Riesling and Sylvaner, the Müller-Thurgau, is often known as the Riesling x Silvaner, but this name is not permitted in Germany. There are also many wholly erroneous grape variety names which include the word Riesling, but which have nothing whatever to do with it: for example, the so-called Schwarzriesling is the Müllerrebe. However, the serious student of German wines will soon be able to register the bouquet and flavour of the real Riesling, one of the great wine grapes of the world and maker of some of the greatest of all wines.

Until quite recently the **Sylvaner** grape was almost as popular as the Riesling. Its origin is uncertain but could have been in the Balkans — from Transylvania. It has been grown in Germany for centuries. Somewhat more luscious in appearance than the Riesling, with large, dark green leaves, it produces bigger berries, which are pale green. It also matures earlier and gives a heavier yield, even in a medium or bad year, so it is extremely useful commercially. At one time, the Riesling and Sylvaner ran neck and neck in popularity and acreage. Now various new varieties are available, maturing early and yielding in abundance, with the result that the plantations of Riesling are limited to those places where they excel without rival; this has happened to the Sylvaner as well, although to a lesser extent.

Another very traditional grape is the **Traminer,** called originally after a small village in the Tyrol. It is a more deeply colourful plant producing rather small yellow-green berries, and is somewhat choosy as to the soil and surroundings that it prefers. Wines made from the Traminer have a delightful spiciness. At their best, they are light, elegant and with a touch of definite musky 'grapiness' that is very attractive from the first sniff.

As the Riesling grape will not mature properly unless the weather is right, there have been many attempts to raise by cross-pollination a vine which has all the advantages and qualities of the Riesling but at the same time will mature earlier and be less sensitive to cool and rainy weather. The trend of cross-pollination has become widespread and there have been surprising results, mixed with disappointments when, after a series of try-outs over years, a promising new species shows serious drawbacks both as regards the vine and the resulting wine. Experiments in cross-pollination are still continuing, rather more cautiously, but the scientists have probably been encouraged to keep on by the extraordinary success story of the **Müller-Thurgau** grape.

Müller came from the Canton or Department of Thurgau in Switzerland. He raised the grape which was called after him in the 1880s, probably as a cross-pollination of Riesling and Sylvaner or, as some experts now assume, Riesling and Riesling. German producers had great doubts originally about the value of this grape and believed that it was a 'Massenträger' or quantity producer only. It was not until the 1920s that more and more growers decided to give the Müller-Thurgau a trial. Once a vineyard was properly established and growers had had the opportunity to follow the development of the wine from various vintages and over a number of years, they found to their pleasant surprise that the Müller-Thurgau produced very good quantities of a very enjoyable wine under almost any weather conditions. They had found a wine with flavour, light, elegant, fruity and with just a touch of what might be termed Muscatel flavour — although there were no Muscatel grapes involved. In a bad year the wine made by the Müller-Thurgau proved more acceptable than that of the Sylvaner or even the Riesling, though it had not the body and character of the latter nor its staying power. But here at least was a wine which, either by itself or in a blend with others, was able to raise the level of the average quality in difficult conditions. It is easy to recognise plantings of Müller-Thurgau, because, seen from a distance, the vines have a fluffy look, quite unlike the rigid rows of the Riesling.

The **Scheurebe,** or 'Scheu grape', developed by a man of the same name, Georg Scheu, of the Regional Institute for Viticulture at Alzey, was raised in 1916 in Germany from a Sylvaner/Riesling crossing. This species excels by its powerful bouquet and generally fruity character: Scheurebe wines, which demonstrate almost a whole flower garden of fragrance, can be almost overpowering in a good year. For this reason, the Scheurebe is grown much less than the Müller-Thurgau but it has certainly acquired a firm place in German viticulture. Unlike the Müller-Thurgau, the Scheurebe needs rather careful handling, as, under certain climatic conditions and from certain vineyards, it can develop an almost metallic taste. But if properly vinified, particularly in a great year, the wines can be great stayers and will develop entirely predictably.

The greatest charmer amongst the newcomers, however, is the **Siegerrebe**, which was also raised by Scheu between the wars. Its wines have a most elegant flower tone both on nose and palate, which matures very well. It has been described as 'all lightness and scent', with sufficient but not noticeable acidity and no notable sweetness. It shows even better in a medium or even off vintage, because it ripens very early. This is the reason why it is rarely successful in a great year, as it is difficult to harvest all by itself, almost weeks before the main vintage.

Another established newcomer is the **Morio-Muskat** grape, raised by Peter Morio, who was for many years manager of the Bavarian Federal Research Institute for Viticulture. It is endowed with a very strong Muscat flavour. This variety makes wines of a flavour normally too pronounced for them to be used by themselves but they can be a welcome addition to a blend of wines from the Rheinhessen and Palatinate where, in an ordinary year, a slight touch of pleasant spiciness is an enhancement.

There are also quite a number of grape varieties from other countries to be found in Germany. The **Pinot Gris** or **Ruländer,** also sometimes referred to as **Grauburgunder, is a classic,** also used to quite an extent in Alsace on the other (French) side of the Rhine. It takes its name from the merchant Ruländ, who first planted it in 1711. Its wines show quite well in Germany, being fruity, perhaps somewhat flat and certainly not possessing the range of qualities of wines made from the Riesling. The **Pinot Blanc,** a white Burgundy grape superbly successful in Burgundy, is less forthcoming in Germany. Surprisingly, it is very successful in certain areas where many traditional German grapes do not really thrive, so the growers' ingenuity may well find further use for it.

Other grapes that may now be found in German wines include the **Kerner,** recently made from a crossing of Trollinger and Riesling and probably named after Justinus Kerner (1786-1862), a poet and a senior official in the town of Weinsberg. It was developed by the Weinsberg National Institute for Educational and Experimental Wine and Fruit Cultivation in Weinsberg, Württemberg. The **Gutedel** (see pp 89-90) is thought to have originated either in Turkey or even ancient Egypt, where it seems to have been mentioned as early as 2,800 BC. Later it was introduced to France and, subsequently, to Germany.

The **Portugieser** vine has nothing to do with Portugal, but originated in the Austrian-Hungarian regions, where it was cultivated for many centuries; it was introduced to the Rheinpfalz early in the 19th century. Its berries are plum-coloured, with a greyish sheen. The **Blauer** or **Blue Trollinger** is supposed to have been brought by the Romans to Württemberg from the Tyrol — hence its name. The grapes are thick-skinned, reddish to dark blue in colour.

The **Blauer Spätburgunder** or **Pinot Noir,** however, probably did originate in Burgundy, but it is mentioned as early as 1318 in Salem and in 1330 in Affental in Baden; as its name suggests, it ripens late, its grapes being small, deep blueish to violet in colour.

The Vineyard Cycle

The vineyard worker leads a happy albeit often hard life. He has plenty of time to contemplate and to organise and, in the absence of stress and the presence of fresh air, he usually reaches a fine old age. A contributive factor is the litre of 'house wine' which, until recently at least, is part of his daily pay. The grower can pick and choose his time and day for doing various tasks and relies largely on his own judgement as to what should be done when. Only the weather can put him under pressure in his fight against hazards such as fungus infections and insects. A crop can be wholly destroyed by rain, spring frost or hail in a matter of minutes, and during the harvest every hour can be of importance. Grapes must be brought in before the autumn rains start and, once in his yard and shed, they must be handled immediately in order to keep complete control of fermentation and vinification. These two processes require a very strict timetable and it is partly for this reason that most smallholders have joined their local co-operatives, which relieve them of this responsibility as regards wine making, even in the most unpropitious conditions. The co-operatives, too, can make use of the sort of equipment that would be far too expensive for a single peasant farmer, and can call on skilled technical assistance at need.

Work in the vineyard usually begins in February and starts with pruning. To prune a vine properly is an art and the success of the harvest depends a great deal on the skill of the pruner. The usual but by no means the only method is to allow for two 'carriers' — the branches that are to bear most of the grapes — one long and one short, also taking into account the way the vine is trained, the incline of the slope, and local traditions, most of which may be founded on generations of experience. How far it is possible to prune both for quality and for quantity is still the basis for a classic debate: on the whole, growers have come to the conclusion that extreme pruning in either direction is undesirable. If the vine has produced too much fruit the plant may not be able to support it properly, although thanks to the enormously strong leaf growth of this astonishing plant this is not likely to occur frequently. In a good year the vine is sufficiently powerful to provide more than enough leaves to support even an over-abundance of grapes, and the surplus leaves are removed during the summer.

Another job for the winter months is the spreading of manure and fertilisers on the vineyard. The vine likes nourishment, but, since it is a fine and sensitive converter of minerals, an unbalanced diet can show its traces in the ultimate wine.

Vineyards on the Mosel near Kröv

The first buds show in late April and early May and are extremely sensitive to frost; there are various methods of overcoming this danger though none of them are really successful. Everything has been tried, from small coke ovens to large smoke-producing appliances, and even water sprays over the vines, on the principle that a coat of ice, once formed, will protect the bud from further damaging low temperatures. In his heart of hearts even the most undevout of growers probably prays to Saints Mamertös, Pancratius and Servatius on three days of May — the 11th, 12th and 13th, for this is the epoch of the 'Ice Saints', after which the greatest danger of frost is past.

FLOWERING

The vine usually flowers in June, but the date can vary from late May to early June in a fine spring, or as late as early July if the weather has been cool and rainy — and, of course, vineyards in southern Germany flower earlier than those in the north. Late flowering will usually lead to a poor harvest, as the grape has not enough time to mature properly. The weather during the period of flowering is very important and can vitally affect the later development of the grape if this period keeps dry and warm. Cool and rainy weather during and after flowering leads to unsatisfactory fruit formation, and, in severe cases, the berries are even likely to drop off.

After flowering, the weather should preferably be warm, with some rain, and the temperature should not drop during the night. A hundred days of sunshine are required from flowering to vintage time, but, in spite of its long roots and Mediterranean origin, the vine does not really thrive in a drought — without adequate water supplies the grapes will not swell.

During the summer the grower will concentrate on keeping the vineyard in trȋm. He will remove weeds and surplus foliage; he will have to spray frequently against fungus infections and insects and he must provide noise signals to keep the birds away as the grapes begin to plump out. A dry, hot summer will keep pests and disease low, but a moist atmosphere may bring on fungus diseases which attack the leaves; the larvae of a small moth may also attack the berries. After a certain date in late summer the use of fungicide and pesticide is no longer permitted and growers are henceforth vulnerable when, with the vintage approaching, bad weather, mildew and other fungi can assail the grapes and may do great damage.

THE VINTAGE

The date for the beginning of the vintage is fixed by the various local authorities but this can vary as regards certain grape varieties, according to their state of ripeness. Red or black grapes ripen before most white grapes, so the harvesting of red grapes is permitted to start well before the owner of a vineyard planted with white grapes is allow to begin his work.

The proper timing of picking is a most important influence on both the quality and quantity, and any change of weather can alter the prospects. Rain can spoil all and make the grapes rot on the vine, but an Indian summer, with warmth lasting without rain until late into the autumn, can still turn hitherto dismal prospects into a good, even excellent vintage.

Ambitious owners aim at quality and will therefore postpone picking as long as possible. They watch the weather from half day to half day so that they may alert their vintagers at a moment's notice to turn out early or late — for every hour counts. A smallholder, however, cannot run any risks in this way, since rain may rob him not only of quality but also of the bulk of his crop. Communes, which try to improve the quality levels of their wines, have always been troubled by the tendency of certain growers to pick early and, in a doubtful year, there may be considerable lobbying from those growers who wish to play safe and want to get the grapes in.

Stages of Ripeness

Throughout August and September tests are made to ascertain the degree of ripeness and the sugar content which begins to accumulate in the grape. A small pocket refractometer, an instrument which shows by the deflection of the light the proportion of sugar present in the grape juice taken from the fruit on the vine, is in general use; it allows the grower to decide with a more than average degree of certainly whether, in a good year, it is worth while keeping some or all of the grapes on the vine even when the general harvest is over.

SPÄTLESE

If the weather remains dry and warm, particularly at night, the grape will reach a fine state of maturity which allows the aromatic fruit particles to develop fully and enriches the sugar content. The product of the vineyard harvested at such a special late date is subject to certain tests and controls and is thereafter entitled to be called Spätlese or 'late selection', which forms the base of a wine very much superior to the more ordinary wines.

AUSLESE

If the grower picks out only the best (most mature) bunches, he will have the basis for an exceptional quality wine, which he is entitled to call 'special selection' or Auslese.

BEERENAUSLESE

It is during these special weather conditions after the main vintage that a fungus which, in a bad year, can be a great enemy of the vine, becomes its best friend. This fungus or form of rot, botrytis cinerea, lives on the stem and skin of the grape and, in cold and rainy weather, accelerates the rotting of the fruit. In dry and warm weather, during late fine autumns, this fungus is quite happy to live on the moisture and water content of the now overripe grape, thus gradually dehydrating the berry and causing a concentration of the essence within. When this effect occurs (the 'pourriture noble' of France, known in Germany as 'Edelfäule'), these berries are picked singly and the wine is entitled to be described as Beerenauslese or the product of the 'special selection of single berries'. After careful vinification, they produce an intense, powerful wine.

TROCKENBEERENAUSLESE

In ideal circumstances and on rare occasions, the berries shrivel so much while still on the vine that they assume the shape and look of raisins. The grapes will have lost most of their water content but they retain their fruit essence, so that the result is a wine comparatively low in alcohol but of enormous strength and concentration; harmonious, flowery and superbly beautiful. These wines are extremely difficult to make, partly because the influence of the fungus (similar to penicillin) slows down the action of the yeast cells, which are vital in the process of fermentation. The wine may be called Trocken-beerenauslese: the word 'trocken' means dry, the whole term signifying that the grapes are almost dried up, specially selected and picked literally grape by single grape.

Under freak conditions, a wine can be made from grapes which are actually frozen. In a fine year nothing is better than a fully mature grape, but in an average year an enterprising grower may risk leaving on the vine a small part of his crop, in certain vineyards where he knows conditions are favourable for this type of rare wine. At the first sharp frost the water content in the grapes will freeze and thus turn to ice, but the essence of the grape will remain unfrozen. The grower, who may be watching through the night, calls out his vintagers. At the crack of dawn the frozen grapes are harvested and taken to the press. In the course of time they will produce a fascinating and most unusual wine, full of acidity but at the same time rich in fruit essence and sugar, which will command a high price.

There is a traditional account which has it that the first Eiswein was made when Blücher crossed the frozen Rhine during the Napoleonic wars, but the first written record of Eiswein being made is a little later, 1846. In that year Eiswein was made at Traben-Trarbach on the Mosel from frozen grapes picked on January 3rd.

UNUSUAL WINE NAMES

Regulations today do not permit the use of many fancy names on German wine labels, but, as the terms may be encountered in conversation or descriptive matter, it is perhaps of interest to know a little about these. The most notable refer to the dates on which the grapes were picked — indicative of the lateness and, in consequence, the degree of ripeness.

St. Hubertuswein means that the grapes were vintaged on November 3rd.

St. Martinswein means that the picking took place on November 11th.

St. Katherinenwein is a vintage of 25th November.

St. Nikolauswein is picked on December 6th.

Christwein is, as might be expected, vintaged on December 24th-25th.

Heiliger Dreikönigswein refers to Epiphany, January 6th, the feast when the Three Kings visited the Holy Child with gifts. It is, in recent times, a problem for the authorities to know just how to date a vintage when the grapes are picked as late as the following year, but of course the occasion does not often arise and, when it does, only a very small quantity of wine is concerned.

Other terms, less frequently used but still in existence, refer to historic events, such as the Türkenwein made when the Turks invaded Europe and the Schwedenwein made when the Swedes, under Gustavus Adolphus, invaded Europe during the Thirty Years' War; a Kometenwein means that the vintage took place in 'a comet year'; in the world of wine, this can often signify something of high quality, but possibly the best-known comet wine in the history of German wines was that of 1811.

Very occasionally, a Strohwein or straw wine may be heard of, implying that the grapes have, after picking, been dried on straw so as to shrivel and yield only a small amount of very sweet juice when they are eventually pressed. The Romans are said to have made a fair amount of wine in this way, but it is not likely that it will be found today unless some producer is indulging in experiments concerned with historic wine making.

Then there are the terms that suggest the wine is frightful — the traveller had better not risk using any of these! Strumpfwein (stocking wine) is so called because it is so sour that it would pull together the holes in stockings. Fahnenwein (flag wine) is of such a virulence that one drop spilt on the regimental standard will shrink it — and bring a whole battalion to arms to revenge the slight! Schulwein is the threat held over children reluctant to go to school — it is so unpleasant — Dreimännerwein is a wine that is so strong that a single glass has to be eked out between three men*, and Apostelwein is even worse, for twelve men have to split a helping between them to avoid damage to themselves. Wendewein is a term of the Bodensee, the wine supposedly being so sharp and acid that drinkers have to turn over from time to time when they go to bed, so that the wine does not settle and actually burn a hole in their guts; wines made in Tübingen and Reutlingen in Württemberg are sometimes jestingly referred to as Elephantenwein — because the grapes are so hard that it requires an elephant to manage to crush them.

Making the Wine

The principle of wine making has not changed much during the past ten thousand years. But today we know more about it and can both help the vine and, as a result, improve the ultimate wine.

Mechanical grape harvesters are now past the experimental

---

* Or it may be that it takes three men to force it on the unfortunate drinker!

stage but, though they seem to work satisfactorily in the United States and other countries, they are unlikely to be of use in the majority of the fine wine vineyards of Germany. Many of these vineyards where they now pick mechanically are large and at least tractors can work them; the mechanical picker requires both space to operate and a fairly level terrain. Some of the terraced vineyards of Germany, however, such as those on the Mosel, are as steep as the banks of a railway cutting — no machine could operate on them. The area, too, may be very small; a terrace may hold only a single row of less than a dozen vines and the soil itself can be so friable that a human being can hardly keep a foothold — a machine would tip over. Visitors who make their way up one of the paths in, say, a vineyard at Wehlen or Berncastel, may feel, giddily, that they are in danger of sliding down through the vines on to the road running along the bottom, or even into the river beyond! Certain patches of vines look inaccessible to anything except a goat.

There is no alternative to the hand of man in vineyards like this. So the bunches of grapes are cut carefully and loaded into baskets and hods carried on the backs of the vintagers; then, when these are full, the pickers tip them into nearby waiting lorries that hasten with their loads to the wineries.

Here the grapes are first crushed, to split the skins, then pressed — a brutal word but in fact the presses work quite gently. At all times there is need for haste at this stage and in warm weather the journey to the press and the pressing have to be as quick as possible to avoid damage to the grapes and so that fermentation should not start up too quickly, before the experienced wine maker can oversee and control every step of the operation.

PRESSING

The modern wine press is quite different from its mighty ancestors, many examples of which can be seen in museums, notably those of Speyer and Kloster Eberbach (qv). In the past, when sheer strength alone was used, a huge beam, with an enormous screw, was the means whereby the juice was extracted by several men straining to push round the gigantic wooden bar. The old wine press was generally an upright wooden cylinder, of impressive design, frequently decorated with intricate and beautiful carvings. These old presses look magnificent, but they were slow in operation — speed is important at this stage in the making of wine — and were difficult to keep clean. Wood can harbour elements that can infect the wine and, if part of a press breaks down or simply rots with use, it is difficult to repair. The grape juice and the young wine is vulnerable to infection at this period of its life and the presses of "the good old days" probably made a lot of bad wine.

The modern grape press is usually horizontal and made of steel. The somewhat sausage-like shape contains a bag that inflates, gently squeezing the grapes to a controlled pressure; this permits the pressing to be quick and speeds up the disposal of the pressed-out skins and stalks, which may be used for industrial alcohol by subsequent hard pressing and distillation, or else sold for animal food.

The juice, or must as it is called at this stage before fermentation gets under way, is then run or pumped into large fermentation vessels, which are secured by a one-way pressure valve, allowing the pressure that builds up inside the vat to escape without letting any of the outside air in. During fermentation, a lot of gas is given up and the liquid bubbles furiously.

The temperature of the must is taken at once for record purposes, as well as to ascertain the degree of sugar, fruit acidity and extracts in it. The degree of sugar defines the ultimate alcoholic content and is essential for the classification of quality to which the wine is to be entitled by law, providing that its bouquet and flavour subsequently confirm the preliminary analysis. The way in which this sugar content is expressed is in degrees Öchsle (see pp 42-3).

When the grape has not had enough time to ripen fully, due to bad weather conditions, there will be a lack of natural sugar within it, causing under-production of alcohol and endangering the wine. In order to make the wine stable, the maker is entitled by law to add sugar to the must in strictly defined quantities, so as to raise the ultimate alcoholic content and make the wine both stable and acceptable; it is essential to bear in mind that this additional sugar acts only as an alcoholic life-saver — it cannot change the fruit essence or the fundamental taste and style of the wine (see also p 45).

FERMENTATION

Fermentation is a chemical process of great complexity and, even today, it is not fully understood. The ever-present yeast cells feed on the must, which provides them with ideal living conditions. Today, special strains of yeast are introduced, which multiply enormously. The yeast cells produce enzymes which split the grape sugar into alcohol and carbon dioxide or carbonic acid (CO_2) and it is this CO_2 gas that will escape through the pressure valve on the top of the fermentation vessel or vat. Carbon dioxide is not toxic but, being heavier than air, will slowly fill cellars where fermentation is taking place, building up from the bottom and thus gradually making breathing impossible. Ventilation of an adequate kind is therefore essential — vital in fact, and serious accidents, when people are overcome by the gas, can still occur if the requisite safety precautions are not observed. Workers who run any risks will, if they are wise, carry a lighted candle so that, if it should go out, they will know that the build-up of carbon dioxide is getting dangerous.

Temperature is one of the most important considerations for successful fermentation. If it is too high, the must will ferment too quickly, distorting the balance of the ultimate wine and leaving it tired and exhausted. Too low a temperature causes a sluggish fermentation — it can even cause the process to stop — and brings with it the danger of attack on the must by undesirable wild yeasts, which can damage the wine. In many instances it is normal practice to assist fermentation by adding a strain of yeast that is already known to be suitable for both the grape and the particular wine region. It is also important to keep a careful eye on the temperature, so as to control it throughout fermentation. With the help of up-to-date equipment for both freezing and heating, there are many experiments being conducted as regards hot and cold temperatures at fermentation time, but as yet no final conclusions have been reached.

The first and stormy stage of fermentation lasts for between three and seven days. During that time the must is cloudy, almost milky, having a delicious taste, a combination of grape juice and carbonic acid plus a hint of the embryonic wine — but this drink contains far more alcohol than the unsuspecting sampler may realise!

After several days, the new wine calms down and looks brighter and this slow, second stage of fermentation continues for several weeks, until the raised alcoholic level of the wine prevents any further growth of yeast cells; these now drop slowly to the bottom of the fermentation vessel. When the wine has cleared sufficiently, it can be racked or drawn off from its sediment into other vessels, where it remains either until a further racking takes place or until it is bottled.

During this period another important process has taken place. Through a secondary bacteriological action, the original level of the acidity has been slightly reduced and the aromatic particles, which will ultimately determine the taste and character of the wine as a whole, emerge and begin to form a harmonious balance — the whole wine is coming into being.

Most years bring complications of one kind or another and the various difficulties caused by over-fertilisation or excessive manuring will have been appreciated. Up-to-date cellar technique now deals with any faults resulting from extraneous flavours in the young wine. Too much protein in it can be a great nuisance, as this can form a slight haze and split the crystal-clear look of the liquid; this may be cured comparatively simply with the help of Bentonite, a silicate which is used as a filter aid. Here the wine has reached an important stage in its development.

The vinification of red wines in Germany is similar to that of white wines, except that the juice of the red or black grapes is fermented together with the skins so as to give the wine the colouring from the skin pigments and also the tannin it requires. Rosé or pink wines are made in two ways, described in the sections dealing with the regions that make them — Baden and Württemberg.

Casks, Tanks and Vats

Before describing the processes involved with bottling, it is perhaps necessary to clear up some misconceptions about the containers in which German wines spend their lives before they go into bottle. The Editor has pressed me to enlighten both her and those who are still under the impression that all German wines are still made cask by cask. In the past this, naturally, was so — which is why casks bore individual numbers and buyers would insist on buying a specific cask (normally a Halbstück of 600 litres in the Rheingau, a Fuder of about 960 litres in the Mosel and a Stück of 1,200 litres in Rheinhessen). As the wines were made and matured cask by cask, they would, naturally, mature at different rates and the wine from each cask would be very slightly different, for better or worse. But long storage and maturation in cask was a necessary evil prior to the recent scientific and technical developments, which have made it possible to bottle these wines so much younger. German wines today are usually only racked once, rarely twice — for a wine which has been too long in cask can never recover from this but a wine bottled too young will nevertheless mature happily in bottle.

Most quality (QbA) wines are fermented in tanks of various sizes and, particularly in the Mosel, stay in tanks for the rest of their lives. Wooden casks and vats, as they get old, are being phased out and replaced by tanks. The superior estates and certainly the very top ones naturally vinify their wines in wood (casks or vats holding from 100 to 1,200 litres or multiples thereof) but economic pressures are now making it impossible to vinify QbA wines in wooden casks although, once you get to the Auslesen and upwards, small containers of wood are essential. Until quite recently, estates such as the Staatsweingut at Eltville offered their average wines, such as Steinberg, by the individual Halbstück (600 litres), each one individually numbered. This practice has now completely disappeared and Steinberger Kabinett and even Steinberger Riesling Kabinett and Riesling Spätlese are offered without bearing individual cask numbers — because in fact they have been fermented and

Traditional method of storing wine in wooden casks

vinified in large containers. True, they have thereby lost a certain amount of their individual cachet, but they have gained enormously as regards sheer economics — which means price to the consumer — and they have fallen into line with modern marketing methods.

So whatever may previously have been believed and whatever other people have written, it must be accepted that, in Germany today, the development of wine in smaller-sized casks is something exclusive to the superior estates and, even there, may be reserved for their top quality wines only.

Bottling

In January the wine has usually finished its first stage of development, although in good years this process can take longer, particularly in wines with high extract (the total of solids remaining after distillation). Normally February/March is the time for classifying the character of the wines and, by April/May, most will be ready for bottling.

To be able to bottle early is the greatest achievement of contemporary cellar technique and the outstanding example of how science has helped to make wine better. Until recently, it was quite impossible to get a wine bright and clear without putting it through the frequently repeated process of racking from one cask to another, usually with an interval of six months in between. This procedure puts a great strain on the wine, ages it before its time and makes it tired. Delaying bottling also increases the cost of keeping the wine in the winery or wherever it is.

Today, the wine maker is able to get the wine ready for bottling six months after the vintage. He is assisted by almost purely mechanical means, such as the use of the centrifuge (which helps clarify the must and wine) and filters (which remove microscopically small yeast cells and thus stop secondary fermentation and other troubles. They also eliminate those 'flyers' whose presence so offended our ancestors that they had to use tinted wine glasses). He has learned, too, to keep the wine as far removed as possible from contact with its eternal enemy — the oxygen in the atmosphere. If air is allowed to get to the wine during any stage of vinification, such as fermentation or racking, then the wine will lose its freshness, becoming tired and flat and likely to acquire a somewhat deep colour — almost amber in tone. It is then said to be 'oxidised'. The traditional way to prevent this is by using sulphur dioxide, SO_2, as an anti-oxidant; at the same time, SO_2 acts as a mild fungicide and reduces enzymes — you might say that it performs the function of a disinfectant. Derivations of SO_2 are present in the human body and, if this sulphur dioxide is added to the wine in an appropriate manner, it can do no harm; over-sulphuring will give the wine the typical 'sting' of SO_2 on the nose and palate and will make it less desirable as a drink, though in no way harmful to the drinker.

Wineries today also use their modern freezing equipment to get rid of the crystallised deposits of tartaric acid, which is the major fruit acid of the grape. In certain years, and especially if the wine is exposed to cold, this is inclined to become insoluble and form a deposit at the bottom of the bottle or on the cork, which looks rather like an accumulation of sugar crystals. There is nothing harmful about this deposit, but the public does not like it and wines that throw tartrates tend to attract complaints from customers. In former times, wine makers tried to overcome this problem by opening their cellar doors in winter, thereby exposing the wines in cask to the low temperatures outside, so that the crystals would fall to the bottom of the cask: extreme cold precipitates the crystals. Today, the wine maker can imitate this procedure more comfortably simply by using whatever freezing arrangements he has installed.

The advantages of early bottling, as compared with the older method, are enormous. Not only is there a considerable saving in labour and keeping costs, but the development of wine in large containers, where it matures in bulk, and even in smaller wooden casks, is something that cannot be carried on indefinitely; the wine reaches a peak and, if kept any longer, may lose in quality. Once in bottle, the wine will develop more slowly and satisfactorily and the onset of its old age will be postponed. If a wine should be bottled too early, the fault will correct itself in the course of time.

Modern bottling techniques are simple but impressive. The wine is pumped from the vats where it has been maturing, through powerful filters, which will eliminate all remaining impurities, including yeast cells, which can harm it if allowed to remain. Then, automatically, the bottles are filled, corked, labelled and sometimes even packed and stored ready for despatch when they shall be required. The whole operation is as aseptic as an operating theatre and all equipment is sterilised (by steam) before use. Apart from the claims of hygiene, the reason for this clinical cleanliness is that the unfermented sugar in the wine will be attacked by alcohol-resistent strains of yeast which, if not eliminated (and yeast cannot live except in the right atmosphere and temperature) may cause secondary fermentation, which means trouble. For, while this secondary fermentation is welcome when sparkling wine is being made, it is entirely undesirable in still wines; it not only changes their character completely but makes them unacceptable to the consumer, unless they are re-processed at vast expense.

COLD AND HOT BOTTLING

This is a subject still much under discussion. But the student of German wines will probably hear it mentioned, so it is only fair to give a little space to it.

The cold sterile bottling method, developed in the 1930s, has proved most successful, but it does take time and there can be mechanical breakdowns which further complicate the process. A cracked filter plate or a faulty pipeline — not always easy to spot immediately — can admit the troublesome yeast cells and their presence may not be detected until later on in the bottling. So large-scale bottlers of inexpensive and medium grade wines have adopted a completely different method.

For this, the hot bottling method, the wine is quickly heated up, via a heat exchanger, to about 49-55°C and then allowed to cool to normal temperature. The heat will kill any yeast cells, and, if properly handled, the process should not give the wine any extraneous burnt flavour. But, unavoidably, there is a distinct loss of bouquet and the method can result in a complete halt in the wine's development, even though the basic quality of the wine is maintained. It should thus be borne in mind that at present fine wines are practically never hot bottled, for to subject them to this procedure would affect both their quality and future development for good.

It is usually possible to recognise a hot bottled wine because there will be a larger than usual air space, or 'ullage', between the level of the wine and the cork or stopper. This has been caused by the shrinkage of the volume of wine, which might have filled the bottle when hot, and which has contracted as it cooled.

AGEING IN BOTTLE

German wines benefit greatly from maturing in bottle. Having come to their peak early and recovered from the ordeal of being bottled, most of them can be drunk with great pleasure by the drinker from nine months after the vintage — some of the lighter wines even earlier than this. But harmony and a true marriage of scent and aroma take time to develop. It is a wonderful thing to follow a wine through the stages of its life and even more instructive to compare wines from the same vineyard from different vintages.

Wines of light character, such as many from the Mosel, give immense pleasure when they are drunk young, will retain their elegance — though perhaps not quite their youthful freshness — for at least three or four years after the vintage. The district, the grape variety, the type of year and the quality of the wine in general are the factors which will determine the rate of maturation and the approximate lifespan of the wine.

Average German wines of quality in average years are usually at their best within one to two years of their vintage. The development of the finer wines goes on much longer than this. For, these days, wines remain younger longer and I think it is true that the consumer has acquired a liking for elegant, stylish wines that have passed through the restlessness of youth. It should be remembered that, although the sweetness and sugar content do not alter with age, the fruit and aroma will develop and increase, so that these two characteristics balance the more obvious ones and the wine's sweetness will thereby be offset, so that it may appear slighter dryer as it gets older.

Great wines from great years naturally start off with a high degree of sugar, but they all follow this 'balancing' rule. The rich wines of 1953 and 1947, almost too sweet to be used as accompaniments to food, showed their great integrity and beauty after ten or fifteen years, when the fruit and the aroma caught up with the sweetness, achieving complete harmony. In 1959 and 1971 the wines had more fruit at the outset and therefore became drinkable at an earlier stage. The great Beerenauslesen and Trockenbeerenauslesen, ultimate achievements of the wine maker's art, must also be viewed from this angle of sugar and extract: they make great drinking a year

after their vintages, but only become really superb wines years
later, after they have had time to integrate in a harmonious
way.

Glass, being inert, is the ideal container — not only as a bottle,
but as a liner for storage vats.

Cork is still the ideal closure, firm and elastic, as long as the
bottle is kept recumbent and the wine keeps the cork wet.
Providing that a good cork of sufficient length is used, there
should be no need to re-cork any German wine, even after
thirty years.

Inexpensive wines for quick turnover, particularly those that
have been hot bottled, are now sometimes stoppered with
crown corks (the type used for stoppering various fizzy drinks)
or spin-on metal closures. These are perfectly satisfactory for
wines intended for immediate consumption. There are also tin
or alloy foil closures for wide-necked short bottles, but it
remains to be seen whether these will continue in use.

Mosel wines are usually bottled in dark green glass, others in
dark amber, all of an elegant fluted shape. The exception is the
Franconian Bocksbeutel (see p 86). But, in line with the trend
towards uniformity and under pressure from the US market, it
seems likely that, in the future, German wine bottles will have
to have a content of 75 centilitres. As, up to now, they have
been only 70 or 72 cl., the bottle will have to be enlarged and it
is to be hoped that its graceful traditional shape will not
thereby by distorted.

Glasses

Any visit to a museum will enable the tourist to view several
examples of fine glasses. The German glassworks — those of
Bohemia and Silesia used to be especially famous — have been
making these since comparatively early times. The Romans are
supposed to have brought the art of making glass to Germany.

For obvious reasons, the examples of glasses that have
survived tend to be the ceremonial type of goblet or 'pokal', a
large drinking vessel, often with a cover or lid, standing on an
elaborately decorated stem, with ornamental engraving on the
bowl of the glass, the stem and foot, plus additional decorative
motifs in relief. The most distinctive of these motifs are the
'noppen', raised clusters of little globules, which English writers
on glassware term 'prunts'; because so many of them resemble
raspberries which have been applied to the surface of the glass,
they are termed 'raspberry prunts' in catalogues. These
impressive, heavy, very elaborate goblets would have been used

for the official welcoming drink, offered to an honoured guest and, frequently, shared between the host and the more important diners in the manner of a loving-cup. When filled with wine, they would certainly require two hands to lift them and sometimes, therefore, they have handles or at least some form of grip at the sides.

The most important type of historic German wine glass is the 'römer', which, because of the way it is pronounced, is often rendered in English as 'rummer', although it has nothing whatever to do with rum — the name is probably of Flemish origin. Each region of Germany tended to make an individual type of this form of glass but, in general, it is a shallow bowl, with a ridged foot which is decorated with several rings, which may be elongated into a stem, this stem sometimes being decorated with prunts, more rings, or a knob in the middle. Various shades of green or yellowish-green glass were used to make the römer.

The fairly straight up and down type of glass, which may sometimes resemble a slightly concave barrel, is known as a 'humpen', or 'brimmer' in English. They too are often intricately decorated, with colouring as well as engraving and chasing and cutting on the glass. Although they look as if they might have been meant to hold wine intended to be tossed off rather in bulk, they were also of importance for ceremonial occasions. The humpen is particularly traditional in Bavaria and Saxony.

These, however, are historic glasses. Today, there are different kinds of glass that the traveller is likely to find. The first, for many tastings or informal gatherings, may be a type of small tumbler; this is the type of glass that is sold at many wine fairs or similar celebrations, sometimes with a device relevant to the circumstances printed on it.

Then there are the glasses used in many instances for sparkling wine — Sekt — which have a bowl of vaguely triangular shape, standing on a fairly tall stem.

The glasses used in most catering establishments will be otherwise: smallish, bulbous bowls on a tall stem, the colour of this stem sometimes being tinted brown for the wines of the Rhine and its associated areas, and a green stem for Mosel. This is the type of glass which is best known to the Anglo-Saxon world as a 'hock' glass; although the variations are many, the essential shape is the same. Our ancestors used to have glasses tinted in various hues to conceal from the squeamish the possible 'flyers' or elements in suspension in the wine; many families will today still have these hock glasses, tinted blue, brown, yellow or green, often heavily cut as well. They prevented the drinker seeing anything of the colour of the wine but they protected him from being affronted by the presence of a flyer!

Today, the glasses of this type which are in use are of course plain in tone as regards the bowl, although the substance from which they are made can vary from the cheaper type of glass to fine crystal. It is worth noting, however, that the style of glass from Trier known as 'Treviris', from the Latin form of the town's name, is still widely in use in the Mosel and is special in shape and pattern. It is shallower than the usual type of hock glass and cut with a pattern peculiar to Trier — several bands of crossed signs and indentations that circle the bowl of the glass; all but the least expensive have at least a little of this pattern on the foot of the glass, plus a knob, also cut into facets, on the stem. The bowl of a Treviris glass does curve slightly inwards, so that the bouquet of the fine Mosels can be captured by the nose. If a succession of fine wines is offered in these Treviris glasses, the very finest, it should be noted, will be served in a smaller glass of the same pattern: this, it is assumed, will capture both the smell and the taste of a wine that is so precious and fine that it can only be savoured by appraising a few drops at a time.

Sparkling Wines and Other Drinks

The stimulating effect of sparkling wine both psychologically and physiologically is well known but can only be partly explained by its method of production. Still wine is the result of the natural fermentation of grape juice. For sparkling wines, the still wine is encouraged to ferment a second time, in a closed container, by giving it a dose of sugar and yeast. A simple process then eliminates the spent yeast cells but retains the newly-won carbonic acid gas and additional alcohol, all on top of the original wine. As the fruit and flavour remain unchanged, the final outcome shows a wine heavier in alcohol but apparently lighter in texture and more elegant.

The full process of sparkling wine manufacture is described in the first part of this chapter, but apart from wine there is a wide range of other alcoholic drinks made in Germany, which will also be described.

Beer is excellent, largely the 'lager' type, or bottom-fermented, whilst in Berlin and now in the Rhineland, Düsseldorf and Cologne there is a renaissance of the ale type of top-fermenting beer ('Weiss-Bier' in Berlin) which is served in attractive inns, rather in the style of an English pub.

Branntwein covers a multitude of distillations still partly very strictly controlled by the German Brandy Monopoly, with heavy agricultural and political undertones. But foreign spirits are well represented and the tourist will have no difficulty in finding his favourite whisky, Cognac or liqueur should the attraction of the local products temporarily fail.

Sparkling wines

Enormous quantities of sparkling wine (Schaumwein) are made in Germany and, as some of these are beginning to be popular in export markets too, it is not difficult to get to know them. Indeed, substantial imports of wine suitable for one of the various processes whereby wine is made sparkling are now brought in by German producers: the German liking for these sparkling wines is such that the German vineyards alone could not possibly supply sufficient suitable grapes to satisfy the demand.

Historically, sparkling wines have not long been known in Germany. The still wines — some of them, as will be remembered, being deliciously 'spritzig' or very slightly effervescent, especially while young — satisfied all domestic requirements. The Champagne process was first evolved at the turn of the seventeenth and eighteenth centuries in France, but it was only around 1820 that sparkling wine began to be made on a commercial scale in Germany. The skill of the German wine makers was such that, although many trained in Champagne, they were soon able to adapt the Champagne method to processes that were found most suitable for making their own wines sparkling and evolve other means as well.

Deinhard & Jordan began to make 'Sekt' in Koblenz in 1843. This term, which is often generally used to refer to German sparkling wines (although now it is subject to controls and definitions) is the subject of much discussion about its origin. The picturesque version of the story concerns the great German actor, Ludwig Devrient, who, in 1815 and subsequently, made an enormous reputation by his playing of Falstaff in a translation of Shakespeare's 'Henry IV'. Of course, Falstaff would not have known anything about sparkling wines! But Devrient, entering his favourite weinstube after the performance, would call for 'A cup of sack (Sekt)' still in character and, with sparkling wine just becoming smart and sought-after, the name stuck.

The sparkling wine now made in Germany — traditionally served in a glass with slightly triangular bowl, like the trumpet part of a daffodil flower — is essentially of two kinds. (A third, once the cheapest type of sparkling wine, was made by pumping carbonic acid gas into the base wine. You could tell this type of wine sometimes because the bubbles that rose in it would be bead-sized rather than minute: they would come slowly to the surface and the wine would usually go flat after a short time).

The very finest sparkling wine is made according to the basic Champagne method, whereby the second fermentation takes place in bottle, the gas, which would otherwise have been given off in the vat, being contained in the wine. The impurities caused by the second fermentation in the bottle are removed by turning the bottle head down and shaking it so that, eventually, the deposit slides down on to the first cork, which in due time is removed, carrying the deposit with it, after which a second cork is inserted. The length of time and skill involved in this process naturally makes the end product expensive and it is only worth while if the base wine is really good: the Riesling and some other German grapes do make wine that is ideal for making sparkling but of course they also make very fine still wines — so that a decision has to be made as to whether the wine establishment will find it worth while to make a sparkling wine from one hundred per cent German grapes according to the 'Méthode Champenoise'; this will, of course, be stated on the label.

The majority of good German sparkling wines, very refreshing both to the traveller and for social purposes, are made by the 'sealed tank' method (Tank-Vergärung). This is rather like a magnification of the fermentation in bottle system, for the wine goes into a sealed tank or vat to undergo secondary fermentation, after which it can, in due time, be bottled under pressure; it is obviously less costly and time-consuming to do this. A variation on this is the 'Transvasion' method, whereby the wine ferments in the bottle at the outset, but the disgorging takes place into a vat. The wine is kept under pressure, and bottled again. At present, all Sekt must be kept in storage under pressure for at least nine months.

Although red and pink sparkling wines are to be found in Germany, the majority are white, ranging in style from very dry to rather sweet. Legally, Deutscher Sekt may only be one hundred per cent the product of German wine; the EEC regulations have made things complicated as regards labelling, but if you read the label of a sparkling wine you will be able to find out or deduce its quality and origin. If labelled 'Rhein Sekt' or 'Mosel Sekt', for example, it must have come solely from that region and it will have been subjected to controls similar to those which apply to the still wines. If labelled as an estate wine, such as Schloss Saarfels, on the Mosel, then it must come only from that particular property. If it is merely labelled 'Sekt', this is an indication that it has not been made entirely from German wine.

It is particularly worth while trying the Mosel and Saar sparkling wines, since they correspond closely to the ideal requirements of a Sekt base wine. Remember that the degree of sweetness will also be indicated on the label — 'Trocken', meaning dry, is the one visitors will probably find most acceptable for drinks before meals, but this term should not in any way be confused with 'Trockenbeerenauslese' (see pp 19-20) which means dried berries, not a dry wine.

A comparative newcomer to the sparkling wine scene is Perlwein. This has to be bottled in an ordinary wine bottle, whereas Sekt, being fully sparkling, has to be in a thicker bottle so as to resist the pressure from the gas in the wine. Perlwein is made by a special cellar technique that retains the original carbonic acid gas in the wine. It may be best described as a semi-sparkling wine, which can be refreshing — quite good with a snack meal or on a picnic, if you can manage to pick up a chilled bottle just before you eat.

Here is the right moment to mention a 'wine' made not from the grapes but from apples. Apple wine, the rough cider type, is a very popular drink in certain country districts and particularly in the Sachsenhausen suburb of the proud city of Frankfurt. This hearty drink is basically made by the same method as grape wine, but is much rougher in texture and taste. It is served in large tumblers and has an alcoholic strength higher than most beers, which makes it conducive to garrulous companionship and also, in my experience, to a reasonable hangover. This dry and fruity 'wine' should be tried and tasted at least once, preferably in inns which advertise 'Apfelwein', or even 'Vom Fass' (drawn for each drinker from the cask).

Oddly enough, applejack and distillations from apples such as Calvados are almost unknown in Germany.

The great producers of sparkling wine, (in alphabethical order), are Burgeff, Deinhard, Faber, Henkell, Karstens, G C Kessler, Kupferberg, Matheus Müller, and Söhnlein Rheingold. They all have impressive establishments, many of which are well organised to receive and show round visitors. It is worth while taking advantage of being in the region to see such concerns, as it will deepen your understanding of the skill of the makers of sparkling wine.

Visiting some of the main producers of Sekt

The following can arrange to receive visitors, but anyone able to plan for such a visit should certainly try to make an appointment in advance, preferably through the export representative of the firm concerned. Remember that any such visit will take an hour or more and involve quite a lot of walking; also that, as it is cold in the cellars, visitors should wear or take a jacket or coat even if the temperature is high outside.

Burgeff, Hochheim: No visits in general, but special arrangements can often be made for groups — contact the firm well in advance and arrange the exact date and time when the visit is proposed. It will be appreciated that only in exceptional circumstances can two or three people be received, but firms are usually glad to accept a visit from seriously interested groups, if their working schedules permit.

Deinhard & Co., Koblenz: Regular tours take place from Monday to Thursday at 10 am and 2 pm. On Fridays, tours go only at 10 am. Special visits can often be arranged if the export department is consulted in advance.

Faber, Trier: This firm does not usually receive visitors, but the Director, Doctor Breitbach, can occasionally arrange for specially interested groups to be shown round, if prior application is made in good time.

Henkell & Co., Rüttgers, Wiesbaden-Biebrich: At the time of going to press, there is considerable reconstruction going on in the cellars but, after September 1978, it should again be possible to receive visitors, so inquiries should be made about this.

Karstens & Co., Neustadt: Tours of the installations start about 9.30 am most working days (not weekends), and include a tasting. It is wise to arrange a specific appointment if possible, especially if the visit can only be made outside the scheduled hours.

G. C. Kessler & Co., Esslingen: It is necessary to fix an appointment in advance to see round here, but conducted visits do take place from Monday to Thursday inclusive.

Kupferberg, Mainz: Visits can usually be arranged if the firm are advised, by letter, some time before the trip is planned.

Matheus Müller, Eltville: Although this is among the ten largest installations, they cannot receive visits at the time of going to press. If you are particularly keen on seeing round, it might be worth while inquiring when on the spot.

Söhnlein Rheingold KG, Wiesbaden-Schierstein: Usually it is not possible to show people round but specially interested groups can sometimes be received, if advance application by letter is made.

Other Drinks

As well as consuming huge amounts of beer — German beer deserves a book to itself and space doesn't permit its inclusion here — Germans are big spirit drinkers. The visitor should take advantage of being able to try a wide range of products, many of which are not easy to find outside the country or, at least, outside those areas throughout the world where large numbers of Germans have settled.

Until recently, the basic distillations made by large numbers of small farmer-distillers were subject to rigid controls exercised by the German Brandy Monopoly, or its authorised subsidiaries. But all controls and regulations affecting this type of drink are about to be changed, as a result of pressure by the EEC. The German distilling industry is likely to change, too.

However, the general public is not likely to notice any marked or sudden changes in the drinks themselves.

German spirits come into the category of 'Branntwein', a term literally meaning 'burnt wine'; they may be the product of any distillation either from wine or from a mash — which last may consist of either a cereal (grain) or fruit base. The two most popular examples of these spirits — which are all served in small portions, as 'shorts' and drunk ice cold — are the korn-based drinks and weinbrand. These account for about 50 per cent of the country's total spirit consumption.

KORN (AND KORN-BASED DRINKS)

Korn, which is a colourless liquid, must be made from certain specified cereals — generally rye and wheat, although barley and oats are also permitted. It may seem odd to the US tourist that maize, which an American will refer to as 'corn', is not allowed to be used for the production of korn at all!

Korn is often flavoured by the addition of juniper, or kümmel (caraway seed). In north Germany a very popular drink is 'Köhm mit Bier' — a kümmel-flavoured drink with beer as a chaser. The visitor to Hamburg is almost certain to see this being drunk in vast quantities.

There are many branded varieties of korn-based branntwein, one of the better-known being Steinhäger, which comes from the little town of Steinhagen in north Germany. It is strongly flavoured with juniper.

WEINBRAND

Weinbrand is pure grape brandy. German wines are not suitable for its production, so the German brandy distillers buy their raw material from France, where vast quantities of more suitable wine are made and also, to a certain extent, from Italy, Greece and other countries that may have such wine for sale. Control of these imported wines intended for distillation is strict but it seems at present as if the German Brandy Monopoly is on a collision course with the laws of the EEC. Until recently, brandies distilled in Germany merely had to be labelled 'Produce of Germany' or else 'Deutscher Weinbrand' and it was not necessary for there to be any reference to the country from whence the basic material for distillation — the wine — originated; this in spite of it being required to label brandies imported as brandy to bear an indication of the country of their origin.

The tourist need not, however, bother very much about this. There are many types of brandy on sale, in several quality ranges, so that it is up to the individual to decide which makes the best base for a long drink or which is most enjoyable as a liqueur after a meal. German brandies are not usually matured for any great length of time. The light style and often distinctive flavouring of many German brandies — which may be vaguely reminiscent of certain flowers or herbs, according to the brand involved — can make them at once appealing and extremely refreshing.

There are many firms whose brands will be found in any bar, but one of the big names is Eckes (who make the brands Chantré and Mariacron), whose headquarters is in the Rhineland near Mainz; the firm also markets a white spirit called Zinn 40, which is made from wine plus flavourings. Other brandy firms are Dujardin and Asbach. The latter has distilleries in Rüdesheim worth seeing.

OTHER SPIRITS

A type of whisky is produced in Germany, although there are no whisky distilleries: the product consists mostly of imported Scottish malts, skilfully blended with German grain distillations — this type of distillate replacing the neutralising element of Scottish grain in Scotch. The result is agreeably drinkable. A small quantity of a gin similar in style to London dry gin is also made and rum, imported straight from the Caribbean, also sometimes blended in Germany with locally-produced spirit, is available too.

FRUIT BRANDIES

The peak of achievement is represented by German fruit brandies, which are world-famous. They are mostly made in the south and south-west of the country. For generations distilling of fruit has been carried on in the triangle formed by the Vosges Mountains, the northern Swiss plain and the Black Forest. Each establishment making these fruit brandies will have its own style but the skill of the German distillers is evident.

The regions involved in this production are, of course, naturally well endowed with fruits that grow wild and they are also rich in cultivated fruit plantations. Most of the brandies are made by the traditional method of the pot still, from which the distillate flows as a colourless liquid; variations in the type of still have been made, but in general anyone who knows how a pot still works — by heating a liquid containing a low degree of alcohol in the 'pot' so that the alcohol, having vapourised, may be cooled elsewhere to its liquid state in a more concentrated form — can understand the way in which the fruit brandies are made. It is important to realise that this type of alcohol is a true distillate of the fruit, rendered into whatever form is suitable for distilling; there is no question of combining an essence or concentrate of the fruit with some spirit. Therefore, the resulting distillate is a real brandy, unflavoured and unsweetened except by the fruit itself. The fruit brandy is not usually subjected to long-term maturation, although it can have a few months' ageing in glass containers or large vats; if the spirit were put into wood, it would eventually become coloured by the cask.

It requires skill to make a good fruit brandy, but the delicate scent and fascinating flavour most possess make them very attractive drinks — although they cannot really be cheap, because of the necessity for using only superior basic products in their production. They are very good digestive drinks to sip after a rich meal and, as the range of them is wide, all tastes can be catered for. If you wish to enjoy the particular scent and taste to the full, do as the locals do and have the glass chilled before you drink the fruit brandy.

Fruit brandies must be distilled only from stoned fruit, such as cherries or plums; the fruit is made to ferment and is then distilled, no sugar, water or colouring matter being permitted as additives. Spirits made by this method are entitled to have the suffix 'wasser' (water) on their names — Kirschwasser, for example (made from cherries). With berries, however, it is necessary to adopt a different process, since the fruit is not suitable for distillation in the ordinary way: it has to be infused in alcohol and subsequently distilled. Fruit brandies made in this way can bear the suffix 'geist' (spirit), as with Himbeergeist (raspberry brandy).

Among the best-known fruit brandies are: Kirschwasser (cherry), Williams Birne (William or Bartlett pear — a very popular type), Mirabellenwasser (using the Mirabell plum), Zwetschenwasser (using the Zwetschen plum), and Himbeergeist (raspberry). Among the best-known houses making these spirits is Schladerer, at Staufen im Breisgau, near Freiburg, in the Black Forest, particularly famous for their Himbergeist; they also make a fine Kirschwasser. It is worth knowing that many of the best German kirsches are usually labelled 'Schwarzwälder' — that is, 'from the Black Forest' — referring to the source of the fruit as well as its place of distillation. The cherry trees in this region make a wonderful display when they come into blossom in the spring, but the district is beautiful all the year round. There are several other major distillers established in this region, among them Kammer, and there are numbers of very small producers as well, so that the visitor has plenty of spirits to sample.

A final range of spirits is 'Magenbitter', which are a blend of korn with other essences and herbs. The result is a rather bitter drink, excellent for settling the stomach or counteracting the effects of too much eating and drinking. They are frequently put up in miniature bottles, each usually containing a single fluid ounce, which can easily be carried in the pocket or handbag. There are a number of brands of bitters of this type, but Underberg is certainly the most famous; it is made according to a family recipe and has been in production for many years — it is estimated by Hurst Hannum and Robert S. Blumberg, in their book, 'Brandies & Liqueurs of the World' (Doubleday, 1976) that about one million miniatures of Underberg are drunk every day!

Wine Law and Labels

The introduction of the 1971 German Wine Law was of great importance, but in fact it was only the latest in a system of controls and legislation, all progressively aimed to maintain and improve quality and to establish that what is on the label of a wine provides all the relevant information for the drinker. Unfortunately, as with any set of detailed regulations that have to be written down, many problems arose and the whole system is under continuous revision and supervision, but essentially the new Law has gone far to establishing guarantees of quality. It is not necessary to understand the German Wine Law in detail in order to interpret a German wine label and certainly not to be able to enjoy German wines. But a little knowledge of what governs the words that may be on the label can increase appreciation — of the care and watchfulness of both wine makers and legal guardians.

The Öchsle Scale

At each stage in the making of any wine, controls are exercised and precise declarations as to the amount and quality of the wine produced have to be made. For example, the sugar content, or the 'weight' of the must — the unfermented grape juice before it becomes wine — will be measured. This is done in terms that are usually referred to in Germany as the Öchsle scale, after the man who evolved the system. Ferdinand Öchsle, a Pforzheim chemist and physicist, who lived at the end of the 18th century, worked out that, if the sugar content of the must could be accurately measured, then wine makers could gain some idea of the sort of wine they would subsequently produce. Öchsle (whose name is pronounced 'Erksler') invented a thermometer-like hydrometer, an instrument that, almost unchanged, is still used by all wine producers.

In measuring the sugar content, this instrument relies on the fact that sugar is heavier than water, the gradation of the scale being related to the specific gravity of water. In very simplified terms, if the specific gravity of a must is 1080, this represents 80 degrees Öchsle and, on conversion, it will be found that the must has a sugar content of 17%. So, after the process of fermentation is complete, the wine will then contain about 80 grams of pure alcohol per litre, or 8° by weight.

It is essential to understand that the Öchsle measure estimates only the alcohol content of the wine — not its bouquet, flavour or after-taste in any way. Just because a satisfactory must weight is attained will not inevitably mean that a wonderful wine will result, however great the care of the wine maker. Some idea of the significance of the Öchsle scale, however, may be gained from knowing that, in a middling year, the must weight of an ordinary German wine will be about 70-80° Öchsle. A Spätlese must have a higher must weight, but this varies according to the region in which the wine is made and the variety of vine that makes it. An Auslese has to attain a minimum of 90-130°, and the very top quality wines will reach 200° Öchsle or even more.

The A.P. number

When the wine grower has declared his crop after the vintage, inspectors may conduct spot checks on both his vineyard and cellar. When the wine in the cellar is ready for tasting samples are drawn off and sent for examination to specially appointed laboratories; an analysis certificate is then issued.

Finally, a panel of qualified authorities, members of the wine trade, scientists from research centres and similar organisations, submit the samples to a severe appraisal by tasting, marking each wine up to 20 points, colour, clarity, bouquet and taste all being separately marked. The wine has to achieve a minimum score in its particular category before it can bear on its label its quality grading, plus the official control number, which is its certificate of authenticity. This number, the Amtliche Prüfungsnummer, is usually abbreviated to 'A.P.' and you will see it on all labels of quality wines bottled since the institution of the 1971 Law. It does not appear on Tafelwein or Deutscher Tafelwein (see below).

Types of German wine

German wines are categorised both by origin and by the quality the finest of them attain. First there is **Tafelwein,** the humblest, although by no means a drink to be scorned. If it is just called 'Tafelwein', it may be a blend of wines, including wines from other EEC countries — but not from countries outside the European Community. A **Deutscher Tafelwein,** however, will consist of German wine only. It will also have had to be made from grapes approved by the authorities and produced in one of the five authorised regions: Mosel, Rhein, Main, Neckar and Oberrheim.

Quality wines

One has to be careful about employing the term 'quality wines' in relation to those of Germany, because the phrase carries an exact definition. But of course, this is something that it is not necessary to watch too much if you are appreciating wines that you enjoy — only to beware of should you find yourself on a jury judging them!

Above the category of Deutscher Tafelwein, is that of **Qualitätswein bestimmter Anbaugebiete,** a phrase that means 'Quality wine of specific regions'. The term is often shortened to 'QbA'. These wines must attain a certain alcoholic content, should exemplify both the region from which they come and the grape that makes them and generally meet with the approval of the authorities who appraise them. They must originate in one of the eleven quality wine regions — Ahr, Baden, Franken (Franconia), Hessische Bergstrasse, Mittelrhein, Mosel-Saar-Ruwer, Nahe, Rheingau, Rheinhessen, Rheinpfalz (Palatinate), Württemberg. They can also bear on their labels the names of specific vineyard areas or districts within these, and even named sites, providing that a defined percentage (at present 75%) of the wine in the bottle comes from the smallest of these named places, the remainder originating within the same Bereich. The best-known wine of all in this category is Liebfraumilch, which must be a white quality wine from the regions of Rheinhessen, Nahe, Pfalz and Rheingan, made from Reisling, Silvaner or Müller-Thurgau grapes and possessing a 'mild' taste. It has to pass the usual examination for quality and be given a number. In practice, much Leibfraumilch comes from the Rheinhessen.

Regional definitions

It is important to bear in mind that each one of the German wine regions is sub-divided: the overall wine-growing region is called the Bestimmtes Anbaugebiet, the sub-sections within this are each a 'Bereich', the name of the particular Bereich being appended. The Anbaugebiete are translated as 'specified regions', the Bereiche as 'districts'; within them are the Gemeinden, a term translated in the singular as 'community or parish', and within these the Lagen, which are specified vineyard sites, registered officially as such. If you can envisage standing on a high point and surveying a panoramic view of a widespread vineyard area, you can divide it up into the various sub-sections and, if you can venture a little further into the interpretation of the way the Wine Law works, it may help to know that the term Grosslage means a grouping of vineyards of similar climatic conditions and soil type, the word itself meaning 'large site'; also that an Einzellage means a vineyard with exactly determined boundaries — in other words, an individual and specific site. Each of the various Grosslagen will comprehend several Einzellagen.

All this helps with working out exactly where a wine comes from and, in the reference books recommended on pp 115-6 (and especially in the *German Wine Atlas*), you will find a complete list of all the sites and where they are. But this is for detailed study and, for the ordinary traveller, serves merely to show how thoroughly the regulations are worked out in relation to German wines as they are produced today.

Additional sugar

The question of adding sugar to wines is one that is always under discussion in northern vineyard regions everywhere. Obviously, in a very cold climate, the wine yeasts may require the assistance of sugar other than that in the grape, except in very warm years. The effect, however, should not in any way be to unbalance the wine or to make it actually seem sweeter — the effect of the addition of sugar to the must (not, be it noted, to the finished wine at all) is to raise the alcoholic content; this is necessary if the wine is to keep well and remain in condition. Should the Öchsle degree be insufficient, then the addition of a strictly controlled amount of sugar — like the French chaptalisation — is permitted.

It is most important to bear in mind that, above the levels of Tafelwein and QbA wine, no sugaring is permitted. In former times, the word 'Natur' or 'Naturrein' might appear on labels, signifying the absence of added sugar. The very finest wines are even more strictly controlled.

SÜSSRESERVE

A term that sometimes confuses people is that of 'Süssreserve'. This, which is a small quantity of unfermented grape juice (which must come from the same region or vineyard as the wine to which it is to be added) can be added, if required, to all quality wines in very restricted amounts, just before these wines are bottled. The subject is complex and anyone wishing to understand the rôle of Süssreserve in relation to QbA and QmP wines should study the more detailed technical reference books.

Top quality wines

The finest wines of all come into the category **Qualitätswein mit Prädikat,** or QmP, a term that may be translated as 'Quality wine with a special attribute'. These wines are sub-divided into five types, but all of them must attain a requisite level of sugar in the must, without any addition, and a natural level of alcohol. Each region has different requirements in this respect, relating both to the area and to the grape used, but the specifications are detailed.

The first category of these fine wines is that of *Kabinett,* a term that implies something set apart, an above average wine. Kabinett wines, like all others in the QmP category, are strictly controlled as to their origin and usually even a Kabinett wine will originate from one single vineyard.

Spätlese wines (see p 19) are those that are harvested late and are hence especially ripe, making a particularly elegant fine wine.

Auslese wines (see p 19) are made from grapes that are not only harvested when fully mature, but selected according to bunches that are specially picked out for ripeness.

Beerenauslesen and *Trockenbeerenauslesen* wines (also described on pp 19-20) are wines harvested late — 'lese' is German for the harvest — and made from selected individual grapes, and, in the final top category, from grapes that have actually dried (the word 'trocken' means dry) on the vine, so that the juice they contain is a concentration of sweetness.

Eiswein (see p 20) is an adjunct to this special category, a wine made from grapes that are actually frozen when harvested.

Understanding the language of the label

Many people are deterred from drinking more than the most ordinary German wines because of the apparent complexities of the labels. But in fact the labels provide plenty of information and, if you study them without panic, they are not really difficult to interpret.

One thing that can put people off is the German script — but this is really no more difficult than English Black Letter: adjust your eyes to it and soon the letters and words will become plain. Take one bit of data at a time and put them together later — you will be surprised how simple the procedures can be.

Then, non-German-speaking drinkers complain that the

names are difficult. What they really mean, in most instances, is that some German names look long and, therefore, seem awkward to pronounce. Again, take such names as a chunk or syllable at a time — they will prove to be no more difficult than some of the English names that tend to baffle visitors. Names of people sometimes prefaced by a title or professional form of address, or names of institutions, needn't be any more tongue-twisting than some of the English double-barrelled names. Our titles can be as puzzling as any prefatory 'Graf', 'Prinz', 'Reichsgraf' or similar word that fills up the label and may give the impression that there is something intimidating about the wine in the bottle! So what do we find on the label?

The vintage: This is simple — numbers are an international language.

The region: The various wine regions have been detailed (p 49) and you have only to read off the one mentioned on the label to know the overall area from which the wine will have come.

The place: In German, the suffix 'er' (the genitive form, meaning 'of') is added to the village name — this makes the word longer, but doesn't change it otherwise. For example, Oppenheimer, for the wines of Oppenheim.

The specific vineyard: This is, of course, only stated for the finer wines, but it is no more difficult to remember such names than those estates, domains or several sites in other vineyards. Remember, too, there are sometimes several vineyard sites that have the same or similar names; this is when it is important to check that you know the overall region and place or village. Names such as 'Doktor', 'Herrenberg', 'Altenburg', 'Kupfergrube' are not hard to bear in mind, when you are selecting a fine wine.

The grape: You can look up the details of the grapes (pp 11-16). This sample gives a particular piece of information that adds greatly to the interest of the wine.

The name of the producer or shipper: This can be a long one, but it is of very great importance. Indeed, there are those who, nowadays, aver that it is more important to know the name of the grower and/or shipper than either the vintage date or the overall name of the wine! It is the producer who endows the wine with individuality, for he alone can control every stage of its development, so that his own standards of quality are met and his own resources deployed to achieve his own particular style, as well as his own demonstration of what this particular wine ought to be like.

The name may be that of an individual, such as August Eser, Dr Bürklin-Wolf, Reichsgraf von Kesselstatt; or it may be that of an institution, such as the Staatliche Weinbaudomäne (the

State Domain), Friedrich Wilhelm Gymnasium (the great school foundation in Trier), or Winzergenossenschaft (which is the co-operative).

The A.P. number: This is the quality testing number, by which the wine can be traced and identified, awarded by the relevant authorities (see p 43).

The type of wine: This will give its category, such as 'Qualitätswein' (QbA) or more (QmP) (see p 44, pp 45-46).

The category of wine: This will categorise the top quality wines according to their type such as Kabinett, or Spätlese.

The bottling: In the past there were a number of terms used to indicate this. Today, the regulations have suppressed most of these but the words 'Erzeugerabfüllung' or 'Aus Eigenuem Lesegut' signify that the wine has been bottled where it was vintaged and made.

If you are looking down a restaurant or trade wine list, it is possible that some abbreviations will be used to identify the regions from which the different wines come: Rg. — Rheingau; Rh. — Rheinhessen; N or Na — Nahe; P — Pfalz; M — Mosel; S — Saar; R — Ruwer.

The Wine Regions

The eleven districts in Germany nominated by the German Wine Law as being able to produce quality wines, subject to a tasting commission's approval, are: Ahr, Hessische Bergstrasse, Mittelrhein, Mosel-Saar-Ruwer, Nahe, Rheingau, Rhein-hessen, Rheinpfalz (the Palatinate), Franken (Franconia), Württemberg, Baden. This division has been made somewhat arbitrarily. The quality of the wines in these categories will reach a minimum level everywhere, but the average and highest quality levels vary considerably from district to district and place to place. It is, however, well worth while trying to see at least a little of each of these eleven regions: not only is it easier to get a clear-cut impression of the wines when you taste them on the spot where they are made, but each region is individual and all are picturesque, their landscapes ranging from pretty to breathtakingly beautiful.

The Ahr

The most northern corner of the German wine producing region, itself the most northern wine region on the continent of Europe, is the Ahr Valley. It is of particular interest to the tourist, too, because the wines seldom feature on lists in export markets. The region's principal town, Bad Neuenahr-Ahrweiler, is only thirty kilometres from Bonn, an easy journey for business visitors. It has a casino and is also where the well-known table water, Apollinaris, originates. It is a very attractive spa.

The River Ahr cuts deeply into the plateau of the Eifel Mountains, and flows northwards past Adenau. The first steeply terraced vineyards are seen twenty or so kilometres beyond, near Kreutzberg, where the river turns east. The valley widens towards Ahrweiler, where the village of Walporzheim produces the best known wine of the region. The river then flows eastwards past Bad Neuenahr. The last main vineyard is at Bodendorf, then the Ahr flows past Sinzig and into the Rhine, almost opposite the beautiful town of Linz.

The scenery of the Eifel plateau is impressive, quite rugged and somewhat inhospitable, very sparsely populated. The climate is below average, as the area is exposed to early and late frosts and there is too much rain in the autumn for the grapes to have any certainty of coming to full ripeness.

The soil is volcanic, dark, with clay at the bottom of the valleys. It is this volcanic terrain and the presence of a large variety of minerals in the soil which caused the early success of the Ahr Valley, which is one of the oldest wine growing districts in Germany, in spite of its weather.

For hundreds of years the growers of the Ahr favoured red grapes, but recently the preponderance of reds went back to only fifty per cent, though the name of Walporzheim is still known throughout the whole of Germany for its red wines. The species of vines planted are largely Spätburgunder (Pinot Noir) and, to a certain extent, the red Portugieser. For the white wines there is now also a fair proportion of Riesling, slightly less Müller-Thurgau, and a few other white grapes.

The Spätburgunder grape originates in France and produces a full-bodied wine, with character and smoothness. The Portugieser was introduced into Germany only about 150 years ago. It is very satisfactory as regards its brilliant colour and its flavour but, by itself and without blending, it is not wholly satisfactory.

These red wines are popular enough in their own region, and many members of the Forces and business people who have spent some time in or near the locality have developed a great liking for them, but their shortcomings, due to the climatic conditions, which often result in a too low alcoholic content, were admitted by the old wine laws: so that, the red Ahrs may be blended with heavier and darker Italian wines as stiffeners, although only up to a strictly defined limit. This method of blending is currently being phased out, and it remains to be seen how well these wines can stand by themselves, without foreign help.

Red wines from the Ahr have a character of their own. They possess good looks and some elegance, but little weight and even the enthusiast has to own that they are not comparable with red wines from France and Italy. They certainly have style but if they are drunk outside their district, on neutral ground, such as London or New York, they may not stand up to the red wines from other countries.

The white wines are pleasant. Their character certainly shows their volcanic origin, for they have an intriguing spiciness, rather light, with not too much weight.

If the wines' quality does not hit the highest level, the scenery does. (Most racing fans will also know the famous Nürburgring, south-west of the wine growing area.) The whole district is easily accessible, either by the main road on the western bank of the Rhine or the new motorway running from Cologne south to Koblenz and Bingen. The Ahr Valley, with its picturesque terraced vineyards, makes pleasant motoring and there are many nearby points of considerable historical interest worth visiting, such as the lake and Monastery of Maria-Laach. Tourist traffic on the main roads in the summer is considerable, but, being off the beaten track, villages and houses have kept their original character to a considerable extent and one can thoroughly enjoy wandering about, especially on the 'Red Wine Footpath' (Rotweinwanderweg) that leads for 30km from Lohrsdorf.

The Staatsweingut (The State Domaine) which is situated between Ahrweiler and Bad Neuenahr, at Kloster Marienthal, is most attractive and well worth seeing.

Hessische Bergstrasse

The smallest wine-producing area in Germany is the Hessische Bergstrasse (Hesse Mountain Road). This is a real gem for the tourist to visit. On the eastern bank of the Rhine a stretch of hills runs from south of Darmstadt in a straight line south almost to Heidelberg. Apart from the road from Darmstadt south, the district is well serviced by two parallel motorways which have only a few miles between them. The Bergstrasse, a favourite weekend resort for the inhabitants of Frankfurt, Darmstadt and Mannheim, rises steeply from the Rhine plain and levels off slowly towards the east. Protected thus against cold winds, it is a superb spot for fruit trees and, on its southern slopes, for vines. Around the highest hill, which is called the Melibocus, are most attractive walks through thick forests or you can go back to the plain which, in spring, will take you through dazzling clouds of pink and white flowering fruit trees. This romantic region is known for its legends and its associations with the Nibelung saga, the stories which Richard Wagner used for his huge music drama, 'The Ring of the Nibelungs'. The villages along the Bergstrasse, including the two towns of Heppenheim and Bensheim, are unspoilt and pleasantly hospitable — again, it is easy to linger here.

The vineyards begin in Heppenheim, which is also known for its fine nursery gardens; there is a largish vineyard belonging to the Staatsweingut, which traditionally offers the visitor both a welcome and a small tasting. The northern limit of the vineyards is Zwingenberg.

Apart from the Staatsweingut, most vineyards are owned by smallholders still preferring to vinify their wines themselves, but the growth of the co-operatives is certainly noticeable here.

There is not much red wine made, the majority being whites from the Riesling and Müller-Thurgau grapes. The wines are pleasantly light in character, and visitors may be reminded of Mosel wines or a light Rheinhessen when sampling them. Most are consumed locally, by bold tourists and the locals, so that very little is left to find its way further afield.

As could be expected, the soil varies considerably. There is granite, sandstone and slate, all of which retain heat to a considerable extent on the higher slopes: nearer the plain, a somewhat lighter soil is well watered by the above-average rainfall.

The Mittelrhein

The Rhine is one of the great historic highways of Europe. This mighty river imposes its image on every type of scenery. It exudes strength and power by the sheer volume of water carried along at great speed between banks that frame the dominating flow.

This impression of power and importance is heightened in the Rhine Gorge, which is between Bingen and Koblenz. The river traffic here is probably the heaviest in Europe: luxurious pleasure steamers of enormous dimensions, freight barges fully loaded and almost awash, carrying merchandise to and from Switzerland, France, Germany and Holland, all form a continuous line of traffic up and down stream. In addition, there are two main roads on each side of the river, two main railway lines, and, a few miles distant, two motorways, thus making this the most lengthy concentration of economic and technical activity, all surrounded by superbly beautiful scenery. It also means that this region is never particularly quiet — so light sleepers should seek accommodation slightly outside it.

The Mittelrhein or Middle Rhine district starts just south of Bonn, and takes in both sides of the river, where there are a number of vineyards sprinkled both on the somewhat flat western side of the river as well as on the foothills of the Seven Mountains (Siebengebirge) that back Königswinter on the east. This is a countryside full of legends, including many involving caves of dragons, and, certainly in years gone by, there was a local wine called Dragons' Blood.

At the beginning of the Rhine Gorge, south of Koblenz, vineyards can only be planted on the southern slopes, depending on the angle of the sun, which is easily obstructed by the many rocky promontories. Wherever there is room between river and slope, the quaint houses sheltering below the feudal castles or their ruins make attractive places to visit. Past the 'Pfalz', or stronghold, which is built right in the middle of the Rhine at Kaub, both the famous medieval town of Bacharach and the Lorelei Rock make a feast for the eye and the imagination. The Lorelei was the beautiful maiden who, from her rock, lured fishermen to their doom. This scenic banquet continues right down to Bingen and Rüdesheim.

The Mittelrhein district stops upstream of Kaub and north of Lorch on the eastern bank, while on the western bank it continues south as far as Trechtingshausen, which is almost opposite Assmannshausen (known for its red as well as its white wines), just north of Bingen.

Space on the ground is very limited here so most vineyards in the Mittelrhein district, particularly in the Rhine Gorge, have to be terraced, in order to make the most of what soil there is. Terracing is a most expensive way of growing vines, but nothing else could be grown here. This contribution to the economy of the smallholder, who largely lives by ordinary agriculture, is a major element in the economic life of the Rhine villages, which are practically without industry in this narrow part of the river.

The soil varies considerably. It is comparatively light, stony, slaty, with clay in the district north of Koblenz. There is really no typical Mittelrhein wine, since vineyards vary so much and smallholders also make their wines in their own ways. There are few co-operatives, which could guarantee a more even quality output. The productive area is exposed to great risks of frost, and the cold air whistles through the side valleys on each side of the vineyards, particularly from the western Hunsrück, causing both mist and fog. Due to the comparatively light soil, an adequate rainfall is essential — but the vineyards are not always lucky enough to get it. The species of grapes here are largely Riesling, plus a little Müller-Thurgau and Sylvaner. No Pinot Noir and Portugieser are grown north of Koblenz.

In this northern district around Königswinter and Bad Honnef, the wines are often not unlike Mosels, while in the centre part of the Mittelrhein the stronger side of the Riesling character comes through, full-bodied and hearty, which is greatly liked by the local consumers and is certainly appreciated by the tourist after a hot day's wandering and sightseeing. The wines are rarely found outside their area and exported only for special purposes and consumers.

The River Lahn is included in the region and it produces

similar types of wine. It is worth while visiting, with its small villages a few miles to the east of Lahnstein, up to the attractive spa of Bad Ems, which was a favourite resort of Bismarck and his generation for taking the waters. It was then highly fashionable and certainly seems to have contributed to a peaceful constitution and long life. The Lahn Valley is pretty, slightly melancholy and peaceful. It would perhaps be advisable to do this circuit concentrating on the Rhine Gorge.

Mosel-Saar-Ruwer

A gifted writer, Rudolf G. Binding, called one of his books 'Mosel-Fahrt aus Liebeskummer', or 'A Mosel Journey to Cure a Broken Heart'. A 'pilgrimage in the Mosel in order to recover from a love affair' is exactly the way one might describe the soothing influence and charm of this delightful river, gentle, amusing, wistful, and certainly superbly picturesque. It snakes its way north-east from the Luxemburg border, with clear unpolluted water, past ever-changing cliffs and hills and sleepy villages, to join the Rhine at Koblenz. Along its banks there are vineyards wherever there is room to put down a single stake on a handkerchief-sized plot. It is a peaceful scene, with the road changing over from side to side of the river, and with the occasional sight of a railway line which, as it simply cannot follow the river throughout its winding path, from time to time has to take a short cut through the hills.

The description of the region as Mosel-Saar-Ruwer, from the names of the three rivers, is clumsy but probably explainable from the fact that the landscape is similar albeit not identical in all three areas; the quality and types of wines belong to the same big family of tastes. In terms of production, this is a very large area. It also produces some of the very finest German wines of quite distinct character.

Parts of the upper Mosel have chalky soil but the rest is almost entirely slaty. The valley cuts through the Hunsrück plateau on the south-east and through the Eifel plateau on the north-west; both of these protect the southern slopes from cold winds. The river itself acts as a heat exchanger in winter and summer, also providing the necessary moisture and humidity when the air is too dry.

The slaty soil of the mountain-like escarpments, where vines frequently have to be both carefully terraced and contained by little walls because of the very steep slopes, gives the whole region its special character. In these surroundings the Riesling produces a wine which is fundamentally light in texture, with pleasant fruit acidity overlaid by an elegant, stylish, aromatic scent, noticeable the moment the wine is poured. These wines have an almost eternally youthful character, due to a slight prickle of carbonic acid gas which is retained in them after fermentation; this gives them a hint of delightful mini-bubbles, which the locals describe as 'spritzig'. The slaty soil here prevents the vine from absorbing the somewhat earthy aroma of other districts. It is their stylishness and elegance, with only occasional weightiness, which makes these light, greenish-yellow wines delightful, stimulating companions on anybody's wine pilgrimage.

A visit to the Mosel requires time; and time has stood still on its way through most of these small villages. It is significant that one of the few efforts to build a new modern hotel in the centre of the Mosel ended in failure — the tourists seem to have felt that it was out of tune with the nature of the valley and preferred to stay in the old-fashioned but hospitable and well-run traditional hostelries along the river. You will not be able to drive fast through the Mosel Valley — it is technically impossible to do so. But you would give up any intention of trying after the first few hours in those relaxing surroundings.

Geologically and wine-wise, the region is divided into three: the Obermosel, (Upper Mosel) from the Luxemburg frontier as far as Trier; the Mittelmosel (Middle Mosel) from Trier down to Alf and Bullay just north of Zell, and the Untermosel (Lower Mosel) from Alf-Bullay down to Koblenz. In addition, there are the districts of the River Saar and the smaller River Ruwer, two tributaries which run northwards into the Mosel south and just north of Trier, respectively.

THE UNTERMOSEL

The wines of the lower Mosel are very pleasant, light, and possess a typical Riesling delicacy, plus fruit; in an average year they are not far removed from the lower ranges of those of the middle Mosel area. In good years, the lower Mosel produces attractive wines though, again, not on the same level as those made in neighbouring regions further to the south.

There are many pleasant villages along the lower Mosel and the town of Cochem with its castle makes an attractive centre to stay.

THE MITTELMOSEL

A few miles further south is the beginning of the middle Mosel, with Alf on the western bank and Bullay on the eastern bank. Here the Mosel begins one of its famous U-turns, at the wine villages of Merl and Zell, the latter famous for the Schwarze Katz, or Black Cat site. None of the tales supposedly accounting for this name seem particularly plausible. The most likely explanation is that there was once a wine merchant who owned a black cat and sold good wines. The Black Cat from the Mosel is certainly a wine worthy of its region.

The village of Enkirch produces wines of great fruit and body whilst those from its neighbour town of Traben-Trarbach are somewhat lighter, more flowery and elegant.

The village of Kröv enjoys the doubtful reputation of having become famous largely by virtue of a wine with a label showing someone smacking a baby's bare bottom — Nacktarsch. This Saxon word is as unrefined in German as it is in English, but it is printed on the label and may, in the pre-permissive age, have given pleasure to some people thus allowed to say it with impunity. The wines, however, are good and certainly do not require this sort of publicity.

Kinheim produces very pleasant wines, fine in character, light and delicate. Ürzig commands a wide area of vineyards and its wines are fuller, fruity, and fine representatives of typical Mosel. Zeltingen produces wines of similar type, perhaps somewhat lighter but not quite on the same level of quality as its famous neighbours Wehlen and Graach where, in the vineyards of Wehlener Sonnenuhr ('Sundial' — which may be seen in the vineyard) and Graacher Himmelreich, two of the finest sites are to be seen. The wonderful wines they produce are considered by many to be the very finest of the whole region.

Bernkastel, with its Bernkasteler Doktor vineyard, towering behind the picturesque town, which it dominates as much as the ruined castle at Landshut, makes a range of some of the greatest wines of the entire Mosel. The comparatively small Doktor estate, by painstakingly adhering to high standards of production and quality control, enjoys a deserved reputation. The actual size of the Doktor vineyard has varied from time to time and only quite recently there have been certain changes in the demarcation lines but it has never exceeded approximately four hectares. The site was originally owned largely by the Thanisch family but today Deinhard have a substantial portion and a little is also owned by Lauerburg. Its wines will always command a high price.

At the time of writing, it is a bottle from this vineyard that holds the world record at auction (see page 96) and it was fifty bottles of a Feinste Auslese from this site that the late Dr Adenauer chose for a state presentation to President Eisenhower. The Doktor's fame may be vaguely associated with its supposedly 'tonic' properties — hence the name — but its wines have always been popular; the vineyard is said to have the highest assessed value of any vineyard in Germany.

The legend of the 'Doktor' seems to have started with the

supposedly miraculous recovery of the Elector of Trier, Archbishop Bohemund II, who, in the fourteenth century was taken ill while staying at Landshut Castle, above Berkastel; however, whatever wine he drank with such good results, it is unlikely that it would have been remotely like the 'Doktor' wines of today.

Incidentally, the two spellings of the name — 'Doktor' and 'Doctor' may be seen on labels; the former, the traditional German, is used today by most owners, and in fact its use was compulsory during the Nazi epoch. However, the Thanisch establishment is unusual in preferring the more modern version.

When considering world-famous wines such as these, the prices they command prompt the question, what determines the value of wine? It must be said that there are two fundamental valuations, when this is attempted. There is the professional, usually in the wine trade, who analyses a wine and decides what it is today, at this moment, and may be worth in the future, as well as what it will taste like in three, six or fifteen years' time. He will back his judgment with his money. The word used here is 'professional' and not 'expert' or 'specialist'; There are many specialists in the wine business who do splendid work and who are also well able to taste. But the great professional is the man who puts his money where his mouth is and is rarely wrong in his forecast about the development and taste of the wine.

The other part of valuing a wine involves the customer — who buys it to drink. He must accept the professional's assurance that the wine is what it should be, that it is well made and that its development is foreseeable on a certain line. The customer must take the professional's word for all this, but what he need not accept is whether the wine is also to his liking. Most people are born with the same physical palate equipment as well as with the faculties of hearing and sight. But being able to hear and see will not automatically make anyone into a Mozart or Picasso, although most people can acquire a capacity to say what they like and what they don't like. This applies to wine. It is the greatest joy for the ordinary drinker to find a wine which will 'talk' to him. It doesn't matter where it was grown and what its characteristics are; once he finds such a wine, he should stick to it and explore the possibility of acquiring similar wines, if possible of the same origin and descent.

No visit to Bernkastel should end without the traveller crossing the Mosel to the twin town of Kues (or Cues), even if only for the fine view from across the bridge. Kues is also famous as the birth-place of the great 15th century Cardinal, mathematician and mystic, Nicolaus Cusanus (von Kues), who

The birthplace of Nikolaus von Kues

influenced all religious thought of his time. He founded the
Cusanushaus, Cusanusstift or St. Nikolaus Hospital, where
thirty-three old men (the number has to be maintained) have
always been cared for. This beautiful building is not easily
inspected by the public but it is sometimes possible to arrange a
visit, which is most impressive. The Cardinal had a magnificent
library — and an equally fine cellar; it is now the storage place
for wines made from the vineyards with which the Hospital has
been endowed and which are sold for its upkeep. The staff are
proud of the antiquity of this great charity sale: say 'Hospices
de Beaune' in the Cusanushaus and you will be guilty of great
tactlessness!

If the wine from Bernkastel does not appeal to the visitor, he
may prefer those from Kinheim, which are lighter and more
elegant. He should not, therefore, force himself to drink a fine
wine from Bernkastel but stick to the lighter types of Kinheim
and similar wines, until he can extend his appreciation to the
others. One tends always to return to one's first love, though,
and this usually applies to wines too.

The village of Lieser has pleasant wines, somewhat light in
character, but further along Brauneberg produces wines of
great character, fruit and body. The Piesport wines are world-
wide favourites which usually attain a high level of elegance.
They are fruity, very aromatic, and are easy to like. Piesporter
Goldtröpfchen, the most famous vineyard, truly deserves its
name — 'little drop of gold'. It is interesting to note that writers
and poets of years gone by speak of its 'golden wine'; the wine
today, however, is not golden at all, being more a lightish
green-yellow. Only Beerenauslesen and Trockenbeerenauslesen

of mature age show a golden amber colour. So there is a sad
suspicion that, in the past, the ordinary wines really were
golden, even amber — but this is the colour of wine subjected
to oxidation, and a fault due to ignorant cellar technique,
which until recently affected the whole wine business.

Dhron produces wines of assertiveness and style, and
Trittenheim has the famous Apotheke site, certainly an elixir
of scent and elegance. The tour here passes Klüsserath,
Leiwen, Mehring and Longuich, all of them making attractive,
high quality wines. The region ends in Trier, an important
historical city, in the centre of some of the greatest estates of
the Mosel.

TRIER AND THE OBERMOSEL

Trier is a most attractive and interesting mixture of Roman
remains, medieval mullioned windows and modern buildings.
Like Mainz, it was the seat of one of the three Archbishops
Elector. The Archbishops of Trier were Princes of the Church,
well-endowed with vineyards and very fond of looking after
them. The Bischöfliche Weingüter (Bishop's Estates), the
Vereinigte Hospitien (United Hospitals), the Staatsweingut (the
State Domain) and the Friedrich Wilhelm Gymnasium (a
'Gymnasium' is a school) each have their offices and cellars in
Trier. They are handsome historic buildings and, if you can
arrange to see round any or all of them, the time will be well
spent. The cellars are impressive and the wines, which support
the establishments, will be labelled according to their origin;
many of them attain very high prices but they do appear on
export lists so that you can revive memories of your Mosel
journey by treating yourself to them sometimes. If at all
possible allow some time to explore Trier — it will reward you
to do so.

The Bischöfliche Weingüter, the Vereinigte Hospitien, the
Staatsweingut and the Friedrich Wilhelm Gymnasium form the
nucleus of estates and establishments in the city who sell at least
part of their wines by auction. As any visitor here will hear
references to what price such-and-such a wine fetched at a
particular auction, it is worth spending a little space describing
what goes on; some general practical advice is also given on
page 96.

For the serious wine-minded visitor, an auction is most
interesting. The only people allowed in are registered brokers
and their guests. These brokers accept buying instructions from
their customers all over the country and abroad; instructions
come not only from the wine trade but also from consumer
associations and private customers, so prices frequently exceed
the limit which the trade is willing to pay. This method of

selling has considerable advantages and disadvantages. The Growers' Association, which organises the auctions, is exposed to great pressure to change the rules and stop the extravagant price fluctuations.

In a good year — when the wines are of top quality — the auction can be fascinating. Some time before the auction there is an opportunity to taste all the lots to be sold and this allows the trade to get acquainted with the products on sale. Then, during the auction, a tasting sample of each wine is poured for each person present, to sharpen his judgment and speed his decision. Each sample of the wines on sale, sometimes over a hundred of them, is carefully tasted, then either drunk or elegantly spat on the floor, with the result that, by the end of the auction, a cloud of euphoria hovers above the heads of the bidders, who are installed at long trestle tables.

The small Upper Mosel wine area from Trier up to the frontier, towards Luxemburg, produces pleasant wines but not of the same class, character and quality as those of the Middle Mosel.

SAAR-RUWER

North of Trier, the valley of the River Ruwer (pronounced 'Roover') comes in from the east, joining the River Mosel at the village of Ruwer. The landscape is attractive, the soil mostly slate, somewhat darker than that of the Mosel. The wines that are made from the Riesling have the same fruit, extract and body as the nearby Mosels but with more lean strength; they are also usually a bit harder. In a medium year these wines may be slightly flat, even dull, but in great years they are very fine, more forthcoming, with good fruit and excellent flavour.

Two or three large estates are particularly attractive because of their scenic beauty: the Karthäuserhof (Charterhouse) in Eitelsbach, apart from its renowned wines, possesses a beautiful park, attractively laid out. This property formerly belonged to the Electors and Archbishops of Trier from the beginning of the 13th century and was run by the Carthusians from 1335 to 1803. Maximin Grünhaus, near Mertesdorf, is a former Benedictine abbey, but the cellars and the aqueduct in the grounds date from Roman times.

The River Saar, the most southern tributary of the Mosel, comes in from the south-east, joining the Mosel a few miles south of Trier. It is a pleasant river, in many ways like the Mosel in miniature. The great administrations in Trier, including the Staatsweingut, have their vineyards in this valley, stretching from Konz right down to south of Saarburg. For all its pleasantness, the district is not really impressive as regards scenery but there is a spell on it, because, every now and again and perhaps only once or twice in a decade, a miracle occurs with the wines.

Compared with the Mosels from the great river itself, the ordinary Saar wines, in an ordinary year, even those from great estates, are scarcely more than just agreeable, being perhaps lighter and more slaty than other Mosels with a pleasant bouquet, but often little more. But a certain combination of heat, sun and rain transforms them. This happened in 1959, 1964, particularly in 1971, and also in 1976. Stately and dignified they certainly are, and then to these attributes is added an almost feline, feminine grace: all suspicion of earthiness disappears and the wine begins to talk to you, demonstrating a weightless elegance, great fruit and delicacy, of enormous charm and nobility.

The great sites are Ayl, Kanzem, Oberemmel, Ockfen, the Scharzberg, Saarburg, Serrig, Wiltingen mit dem Scharzhof, with many famous estates and growers producing wines that, in the right vintage, will be memorable.

Anyone to whom Saar wines have not yet shown themselves in their glory should go on trying them; the ultimate reward will be great. Before an important recent testing in the City of London's Guildhall, eight professionals in the wine trade disputed as to how best to end a showing of ten distinctive and great German wines. While a Beerenauslese from the Rheingau showed superb strength and power, it was finally beaten by a Trockenbeerenauslese from the Saar which, though a lighter wine in weight and texture, gave a scintillating display of grace and elegance.

The Nahe

This is a small region, comparatively little known to most Anglo-Saxons, although the wines invariably appeal to them. The countryside is quite unlike that of the Rhine or Mosel, generally more open and undulating, rather amiable. Our ancestors frequented it because of its various spas, reputedly beneficial to sufferers from a variety of complaints.

Because these springs are generally associated with the vineyards it is perhaps worth describing the way they are utilised. For example, at Bad Munster-am-Stein (the preface 'Bad', meaning bath, implies that the place is or has been a spa) and also at other spas, the authorities have built a high scaffolding, about 30 feet high, 100 feet long and 10 feet across and have put this in a shallow trough out in the open. The local saline springs are pumped to the top of the scaffolding and allowed to drip down over a rough wall of twigs; this disperses the water into fine spray, which is inhaled by the patients who sit in front of the scaffolding, taking their cure. The author of this book, aged five, fell into the bottom of one of these contraptions and had to be fished out by his mother. These saline springs are typical of the Nahe district, for the whole region is volcanic. There are three distinct regions, the Niedernahe (Lower Nahe), which extends from Bingen in the north (where the river Nahe joins the Rhine), almost up to Bad Kreuznach; then there is the most important central part from Bad Kreuznach to Schlossböckelheim, and finally, further to the south and both on the Nahe and its tributaries, such as the Alsenz and the Glan, there is the Upper Nahe. Geologically, all three are widely different as regards soil and are quite unlike the Mosel. On a volcanic base or subsoil there is a layer partly of slate, partly of clay, plus a large variety of different components which make Nahe wines so pleasing and, at the same time, very different from one another.

In the north, or lower region of the Nahe, between the Hunsrück and the Rheinhessen hills, wines of a light, fruity, definite character are made, almost as if they were composed of a blend of Rheingau and Rheinhessen. The upper Nahe produces wines of a much lighter texture, not wholly unlike the Saar wines. But it is the centre of the Nahe district which makes a very wide range of wines from the everyday right up to the top categories. This includes the part of the river valley between Bad Kreuznach and Schlossböckelheim.

No Nahe wine is ever dull. The taste may be somewhat obtrusive as regards fruit, too pronounced in style or too dry, or even too light, but there is always a spiciness to them and it is this that makes them attractive. Nahe wines are not heavy, though sometimes it would be hard to describe them as full-bodied, but what they lack in weight they make up in flavour.

In spite of the comparatively small area, the vineyards of the Nahe are up to date and modern in the way the vines are planted. There are a number of fine estates, as well as Staatsweingut, and an increasing proportion of growers, particularly smallholders, use the co-operatives to help them with cellar work and marketing.

Apart from a small quantity of red wines produced from the Spätburgunder (Pinot Noir) and Portugieser grapes, there are equal proportions of Riesling, Müller-Thurgau and Sylvaner planted, according to the soil and the climate: on the whole the weather is quite temperate and the region is protected from frost. There are interesting experiments in progress relating to new grape crossings, and the wide variety of soil here permits trials to be made under varying conditions.

Any visitor should make a point of drinking a wine from the centre of the Nahe, of at least Spätlese rank, in a leisurely way.

There is a distinct jump (almost more so than in other wine districts) from the ordinary consumer quality to the QmP of Spätlese or Auslese, so these are good wines to help the student register what these categories are like. One may well be surprised at the high level of balance, dignity, elegance, stylishness and the almost exotic flavour which these wines have to show. In some ways, they can be compared with the great wines of the Nackenheim/Bodenheim area in Rheinhessen, and their style — though not their weight — is a reminder of some of the more flowery products of Kiedrich and other villages in the Rheingau. Unfortunately there is also a great difference between average and good years: though this is not as pronounced as it is in the Saar, it pays to abstain from the wines of average vintage years and concentrate on the Spätlesen wines and upwards of the great vintages. These are superior but do not really challenge the weightier wines from the Rheingau. However, they are excellent introductory wines to the giants.

The Nahe is a charming river, comparable in attractiveness to the Rhine Gorge or the Mosel, and more amiable and pleasant than the River Ahr. There is some light industry, and at Bad Kreuznach in particular there are factories that have pioneered both the experimental stages and the production of machinery and equipment essential for modern vineyards, wineries and cellars. Kreuznach is a largish spa, an evocative relic of a former type of holiday resort in a region that, nowadays, would probably be associated more with streamlined modernity. The countryside is well worth exploring, especially as the local publicity organisations are active in providing assistance to tourists who wish to explore the Nahe, both on foot and by car.

Houses on the bridge at Bad Kreuznach

Bingen is a pleasant town with more small, narrow streets than one would have thought possible. It has given its name to the Binger Loch, or the Straits of Bingen, where, with the narrowing of the Rhine Gorge and the presence of rocks in the riverbed, navigation has become hazardous. Recent efforts to make it easier for ships to pass each other on this difficult spot led to too much dynamiting of the river bed and banks, which upset the flow of the river and made things even more difficult.

On a little island in the middle of the Rhine, almost opposite its confluence with the Nahe, is the stark Mäuseturm ('Mouse Tower'), associated in legend with the villainous Bishop Hatto; this Bishop, it was said, greatly oppressed his people and, in a famine, stocked up the tower with provisions and settled in, regardless of whether anyone else lived or died. However, according to the tale (which Southey turned into a poem), thousands of mice swam out to the island and gobbled him up. It has, however, now been established that Bishop Hatto was a real person, in fact a rather well-intentioned ruler, who lived at a different period; the Mäuseturm was really built as a 'Maut' tower, or fortified rendezvous from which officials could collect taxes and dues from the ships passing on each side of it. But the mouse legend survives.

The Nahe valley and its tributaries are well laid out for motoring and the region, which is full of places of historical interest, is approachable either by the main road along the Rhine from Koblenz to Bingen, or via the autobahn that connects Koblenz, Bingen, Alzey and Mainz. How you plan your visit to this delightful region depends on your mood and the time you have to spend.

The Rheingau

The arc that starts by the Rhine at Rüdesheim, goes northwards along the Taunus Hills and returns gently to the river at Wiesbaden, some thirty kilometres away, encloses the greatest array of white wine vineyards in the world. Here is sheer mastery of wine. Every village and estate demonstrates how wonderful these wines can be when at their best.

The Rheingau actually begins further north-west, in the Rhine Gorge at Lorch, and runs through to Hochheim, eastwards along the River Main. In the upper regions the soil is mostly slate but lower down there is quite a variety, ranging from clay to sand. The climate is excellent for wine: the Taunus hills protect the Rheingau from the winds from the north-west and north-east. The land slopes towards the south, enabling the sun to strike the vineyards almost at a right angle. The moisture that rises from the river provides the necessary humidity. The Rhine also acts as a heat exchanger and moderates any extremes of heat and cold that may occur.

The Rheingau is ideal walking country. Footpaths are well laid out and signposted all through the Taunus Hills, with frequent pointers towards the nearest wine village. There are large open beech forests with attractive views of the Rhine Valley and beyond to the Rheinhessen region. Slightly further north, and right in the Taunus Hills, are a number of small villages which provide cool shade in the summer. Tiny flower-adorned spas, such as Schlangenbad and Bad Schwalbach, make excellent centres for excursions. More worldly, with fine shops, restaurants, a casino and an opera house, is the artistic centre, Wiesbaden, which, in spite of having a quarter of a million inhabitants, still preserves its elegant 19th century character, in a setting of parks and gardens, surrounded by the Taunus Hills.

Lorch, where the Rheingau is somewhat arbitrarily said to begin, is a pleasant little town at the mouth of the small River Wisper, which runs from the Taunus Hills down to the Rhine. The Wisper Valley consists of fifteen miles of idyllic scenery; it is closed in but is not wild and is bordered by a large variety of trees. Those who like cycling should take their bicycles by train to Bad Schwalbach, push them up to the top of the hill behind the town, then mount and coast down without effort along the Wisper right through to Lorch.

From Lorch south-east along the Rhine, the next town in a similar position is Assmannshausen, resplendent with welcoming inns and hotels, well known as a festival centre and for its superb view of the Rhine Gorge, with its picturesque castles, ruins, and the ever-changing river itself. Although Lorch has no particular claim to making fine wines, the high proportion of Riesling grown there makes some that prove pleasant thirst quenchers after the trip along the Wisper Valley. Assmannshausen, on the other hand, is very well known for its red wines. Two-thirds of its vineyard acreage is planted with Pinot Noir and Portugieser, and the Staatsweingut owns a significant share of the output of red. The white wine, largely made from the Riesling, is perhaps less successful. Assmannshauser red is deservedly acclaimed in a good year and produces stylish wine with body and flavour.

Assmannshausen is also famous for a different reason. It proudly boasts the finest restaurant in the region and probably one of the best in the whole of Germany. This is the Hotel Krone. Local specialities do not steal the scene and excellent classic dishes, including sea food recipes from France and the Mediterranean, and particularly game and venison, are featured and served with meticulous care. It is relevant to note

that wine lists here and elsewhere in Germany are usually quite
adequate as regards the national wines but they are not as
comprehensive as in hotels or restaurants of equal standing in
the U.K. Only a few foreign wines will be listed here and even
the modest ones will feature at high prices.

Now the greatest sites begin, all of them on the north bank of
the Rhine, so that the vineyards face towards the river, getting
all the warm sun — and also profiting from the reflected light
and heat from the water itself.

Rüdesheim, the next town in the Rheingau to the east, can
be approached by two routes: some people prefer to drive up to
the hills immediately behind Assmannshausen, on a very steep
road with beautiful views of the Rhine Gorge, which ends at the
great monument built after the 1870/71 war, to celebrate the
foundation of the second German Reich. This stands on a
rocky promontory, framed by the tops of the hills, overlooking
the junction of the Nahe and Rhine, the Mäuseturm, and the
hills across the Nahe in the regions of Rheinhessen and
Hunsrück. The second approach to Rüdesheim is along the
Rhine. Suddenly the Gorge widens and presents the panorama
of the Rhine plain, with the gentle Taunus Hills on the left and
the slightly sharper backdrop behind Bingen on the right. It is
a friendly, stimulating sight which never fails to impress and is
equalled only by the view from the new Mainz-Schierstein
bridge, high above the plain en route from Rheinhessen to
Rheingau, where the scenery is equally dramatic.

On the way to Rüdesheim, the extraordinarily terraced
vineyard formations are still prevalent, but they are soon
superseded by the more traditional method of planting, on
smoother slopes.

Rüdesheim is a pretty town, directly facing the Rhine; it has
a considerable tourist industry and quite a lot of traffic.

The half-timbered Drosselgasse at Rüdesheim

The famous narrow lane, at right angles to the river, the 'Drosselgasse' ('Thrush Lane') consists almost entirely of bars and weinstuben and, on a holiday, is thronged with visitors. All along the town's river frontage are hotels, bars and souvenir shops, pleasant to stroll past although somewhat noisy as the evening wears on.

Rüdesheim's grapes are almost exclusively Riesling. The wines are good without quite reaching top quality, but they are not heavy and possess some elegance and fruit. The town's enormous number of vineyard names was drastically pruned by the 1971 German Wine Law. (Beware of confusing the Rheingau's Rüdesheim with another Rüdesheim, which is in the Nahe district; this last produces wines of an entirely different character not, in my view, equal in quality to the Rheingau Rüdesheim wines.)

In the ruined castle of Brömserburg at Rüdesheim, there is an important collection of objects to do with wine: equipment, presses and tools of great antiquity, drinking vessels ranging from the primitive to the most elaborate are on display and the different shapes of German wine bottles dating from very early times are also shown.

The neighbouring town of Geisenheim, further east, also grows mainly Riesling, but with a certain amount of Sylvaner and Müller-Thurgau as well. It is here that the famous Wine Institute does so much important experimental work. Geisenheim, with its red soil, produces wines of considerable character which, in a normal year, demonstrate body, flavour, and weight and, in a good vintage, develop into great wines. They have fruit and harmony and show plenty of character.

Geisenheim as a place has been somewhat spoilt by the light industry and a type of town planning in which well-meant modern constructions do not quite mix with the style of the remaining older buildings. This is true to a certain extent of the whole Rheingau, where towns and villages with fine old buildings and historic layout are not yet in tune with modern developments and town planning. Other regions, such as certain villages in Rheinhessen and certainly in the Pfalz, give a more striking impression of harmony and well-being. There is certainly no Rheingau equivalent of villages further south-east, such as those in Baden-Württemberg, or towns like Würzburg, which is a jewel of architecture, completely at home in the middle of vineyards and the surrounding countryside.

If in Geisenheim wines begin to indicate what the great Rheingaus are like, it is also a real parting of the ways, as far as the vineyard tour is concerned. The road leading straight on eastwards arrives at Winkel after two miles; this, combined with its buffer village Mittelheim, forms a union with Östrich, thus

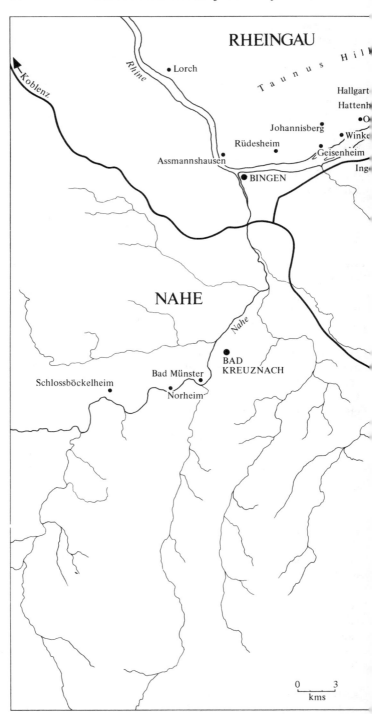

making one long riverside ribbon development, with vineyards along it on the higher ground. The other road forks north-east at the exit from Geisenheim and goes up into the Taunus Hills; after a mile, it bypasses the village of Johannisberg, then twists uphill and comes out on top of the outlying houses of Johannisberg, which is dominated by Schloss Johannisberg; this stands on a bluff overlooking the vineyard slopes and offers a panorama of the Rhine from the Mainz to the left down to the Rhine Gorge at Bingen on the right. Schloss Johannisberg is an impressive building, originally bestowed on the Benedictines in the eleventh century by the then Archbishop of Mainz. This order dedicated their monastry to St. John the Baptist, hence the name of the site — St. John's Mountain. After Napoleon sequestered all the religious establishments, Schloss Johannisberg was owned successively by the Prince of Orange, by Napoleon himself and by the Emperor of Austria, who gave it to Prince Metternich in 1816, as a reward for his masterly diplomacy at the Congress of Vienna. The Metternich family still own the property and their name is therefore given on the wine labels.

There are a number of other fine estates here too. In hilly villages like Johannisberg and further to the east, the soil is much heavier than it is lower down, in the plain; so, in a very dry year, the vine is able to draw sufficient moisture from the ground when vineyards lower down suffer from lack of water. In very dry years it is the hill villages that produce the best wines.

Though most Johannisberg grapes are Riesling, grown on similar soil throughout, the different methods of vinification used at the various estates can produce wines of quite different character. At an auction tasting in the late 1930s, both Schloss Johannisberg and von Mumm, a neighbouring property, showed a large range of the two great vintages of 1933 and 1934. Whereas the Schloss wines were dignified, weighty and full, the Mumm wines displayed more elegance and stylish character, being more flowery but with less weight and body.

The new German Wine Law has converted part of the region into one district, just called Johannisberg, comprising Assmannshausen right through to Wiesbaden, in an attempt (perhaps misguided) to acknowledge that the Johannisberg wines are overall typical of that stretch of ground. It is therefore better for the visitor to stick to single vineyard wines if possible, not only in Johannisberg itself, whether from the great Schloss or Mumm or one of the many smaller excellent estates, which are all fascinating to taste in any year. Many of the wines are weighty and winey, with fruit, body and style. The Riesling grape in an average year can be a bit hard, but blossoms forth with strength and balance when allowed by the weather to gain full maturity.

The little town of Östrich-Winkel, with its pretty houses, is very attractive, albeit partly modern. The wines are very good, reaching the top levels and a number of estates have been enterprising in experimenting with other grape species. Riesling is unbeatable, though Müller-Thurgau, Sylvaner, Pinot Blanc and Traminer have been quite successful. These vineyard experiments are helped enormously by the famous oenological institute, wine school and training centre in Geisenheim, rightly acclaimed for study and most valuable research into all aspects of wine planting and vinification. The great advances in cellar techniques everywhere are, to a considerable extent, due to its efforts. It was at a Schloss or castle here that the ancestor of a very well-known contemporary grower, Graf von Schönborn, drafted the treaty that ended the Thirty Years' War in 1648.

The best-known estate at Winkel is Schloss Vollrads, two kilometres to the north, owned by the Greiffenclau family since the fourteenth century. They claim to be the oldest Rhine wine dynasty and Graf Matushka-Greiffenclau still owns and runs the property. The Schloss itself has been considerably rebuilt at various periods and the library now houses the family museum, but an introduction and prior appointment are usually necessary in order to see this.

Leaving Östrich, the left hand road goes up to another hill village, Hallgarten. This is the home of five great estates, which in good years produce wines of particular finesse, style and elegance without quite the weight of their neighbours. Again, it is mostly Riesling that is grown here and the wines certainly belong to the inner circle of the great Rheingau villages.

Moving back to the Rhine plain, Hattenheim is to the east. It is perhaps the prettiest village in the Rheingau, with its houses grouped in the traditional way and its atmosphere of contented village life. Its wines form part of the crown jewels of the Rheingau.

Hattenheim and Erbach, further east, form the base of a triangle which has its apex at the great Steinberg vineyard near Kloster Eberbach, right in the foothills of the Taunus.

This emerald-studded triangle contains an area of great vineyards such as Hattenheimer Wisselbrunn, Erbacher Marcobrunn, and Steinberg, which all produce wines of profundity and individual character, and the visitor is likely to find some aspect of perfection in every wine he drinks. The Marcobrunn wines were the favourites of Thomas Jefferson, who visited the region in 1788. The spring from which the place gets its name ('Brunnen' means a spring or a well and this one was dedicated to St. Mark) is at the dividing line between Erbach and Hattenheim and each village tried to get possession of the spring. Eventually it was decided in court that it really belonged to Erbach but, after the ruling and under cover of darkness, someone from Hattenheim chalked up on the wall of the spring:

'Erbach has the water —
But Hattenheim the wine.'

Until the beginning of the twentieth century these wines were simply known as Marcobrunn and found in all good wine lists in Germany and abroad. Today it is generally accepted that the wine is correctly called Erbacher Marcobrunn and, if it is not the best, it is certainly very very good.

Erbach and Hattenheim produce wines of similar character; exciting, stimulating, beautifully balanced and polished, with great bouquet and certainly considerable body and weight. By comparison, the vineyard of Steinberg has perhaps less weight but excels with its superb grapey flavour, which is also found in wines from other hill villages, such as Rauenthal and Kiedrich and to a lesser extent in those few exceptional wines from the river Nahe or the Bodenheim/Nackenheim area of Rheinhessen, which are, however, not quite in the same class. More elegance and less weight make these hill village wines almost easier to drink than their heavier brothers which come from lower down the slope.

The monastery of Kloster Eberbach adjoins the vineyard and is well worth a visit. The scenery is superb and the monastery an architectural gem of great charm. The vineyard belongs to the Staatsweingut, whose administrative buildings are in Eltville, but with cellars both there and in Eberbach. Recently

Kloster Eberbach

Kloster Eberbach has become more widely known outside Germany because of an imaginative project run by the official German Wine Publicity Agency, who have organised wine seminars there (see p 97) in English.

Outside the Rheingau village of Erbach, with its attractive church, is Schloss Rheinhartshausen, one of the most impressive and important estates. A luxury hotel and restaurant have been built out of the former owner's home for people who wish — and can afford — to stay and explore. The large island in the middle of the Rhine exactly opposite Schloss Rheinhartshausen is locally known as the Au, or correctly Aye, a water meadow. One meaning of this word, a pasture, is known to Wagnerians — it features in the Good Friday Scene of Wagner's opera Parsifal — but this Au is planted with fine, comparatively new vines, whose wine is entitled to bear the name Erbacher Rheinhell. The grapes are largely Pinot Blanc; they like their new home and have produced a full fruity wine. The effect of the moisture of the river from both sides and the favourable Rheingau climate makes the island rather like a hothouse with a built-in humidifier.

A mile and a half away is Eltville, which is also the seat of the Staatsweingut and other estates, a lively town making good, firm but fine wines. The name of the town derives, not from the French, but from Latin, though why 'Alta Villa' — the high town — should be given to a place on a river is difficult to understand. Two miles further east are the twin towns of Oberwalluf and Niederwalluf. The latter, right on the Rhine, is a charming spot, well known as an excursion place and for its pleasant weinstuben and bars. The wines are good, without great distinction, and they are mostly drunk locally.

Five miles further north, in the foothills of the Taunus, are the three most eastern villages, whose wines are mostly on the same level of quality as those of the villages of Hallgarten and Johannisberg, further to the west. Martinsthal, on the road to the delightful little spa of Schlangenbad, makes wine of body and fruit, though rather lacking in finesse; this village used to be known as Neudorf or 'New Village' but changed its name nearly a generation ago. There are scores of 'Neudorf' in Germany, but whether the change here was made from reasons of snobbery or to stop confusion is not clear. It would be interesting to find out whether this alteration has helped the sale of the wines, though it is possible that the word 'Neudorf' was formerly seen more frequently on wine lists than Martinsthal is today.

Martinsthal is on the road, right in the valley; Rauenthal is on the top of the plateau, and has very heavy soil. In hot summers it produces superb, assertively noble wines. Apart from the local co-operative, a number of estates, including the Staatsweingut, own vineyards in Rauenthal and their wines merit serious attention. In an indifferent year their taste may be a bit unyielding, even hard, but they are always full of fruit and possess admirable balance.

Back to the west at the same altitude lies Kiedrich, a delightful place, wealthy in appearance, with a number of well-kept old houses. It makes excellent wines, slightly more stylish and elegant than those of Rauenthal, with the typical fine, immediately noticeable grape scent always produced by the Riesling when it feels perfectly at home — as it does here. The consistently high level of Kiedrich wines throughout the years is largely due to the inspired vinification of some of the leading estates here and Kiedrich wines are always deserving of serious appraisal.

A picturesque road runs north from Kiedrich to Hausen vor der Höhe and, if the journey is continued northwards through the Taunus Hills up to the top, the difference in temperature is quite startling and demonstrates the considerable shelter which the Taunus range provides for the Rheingau vineyards.

There are small vineyards to the west of Wiesbaden, but they are not of great importance. Above Wiesbaden itself, the slopes of the Neroberg, a hill overlooking the town, used to produce a very good wine, of which the 1920 and 1921 Neroberger were excellent examples; they were sold almost exclusively in Wiesbaden, thus contributing to the attraction of this elegant, amusing place.

East of Wiesbaden, a sprinkling of vineyards extends almost to the outskirts of Frankfurt, but the wines from them are scarcely known under their own names and are marketed either locally or under the district name of Hochheim. The town of Hochheim is certainly the most eastern outpost of wines of Rheingau type and quality. It is a pleasant place, standing on a plateau overlooking the River Main, the slopes below the town falling gently away towards the valley and Mainz. One of Hochheim's claims to fame is as the source of the word 'hock', which is popularly supposed to have originated in the nineteenth century and to have become a more fashionable term than the more general name 'Rhenish' for Rhine wines, on account of Queen Victoria and the British Royal Family making them smart drinks. But in fact the word hock — or 'hockamore', an anglicised version of Hockheimer — is cited by the Shorter Oxford Dictionary as being in use as early as 1625. It was probably brought back to England by the soldiers fighting in the various wars of the time and easily became shortened to 'hock'.

The soil around Hochheim is medium light to heavy and the

grapes are mostly Riesling. The wines are not unlike the hill village types on the other side of Wiesbaden, fruity and with good body, but not very forthcoming in an average year; in a good year they are capable of producing big-boned wines, good fellows, long lasters but perhaps not very polished.

Rheinhessen

Rheinhessen is a vast, dense area of vineyards, one of the largest in Germany. It is probably via a wine from this region that most of us have come to German wines. The region is bounded to the east by the Rhine as it flows north from Worms to Mainz. The river is also the region's northern boundary as it turns at Mainz to Bingen. Its southern limit is a line roughly drawn to Worms from Bad Kreuznach through Alzey. It is a mellow landscape, possessing a good climate, with gentle hills, not as dramatic as those of the Rhine Gorge or the Rheingau in general. Even along the river banks in the north, with the beautiful panorama of the Taunus Hills in the background, the scenery is friendly but not breathtaking. Only after Mainz, as one goes southwards past Laubenheim and through to Guntersblum, where the high plain breaks towards the Rhine, is there more definition and character to the pleasant landscape. High up, just south of Dienheim, a rare view is given of the Rhine and across to the Bergstrasse but somehow, even amongst the more pronounced scenic effects, the overall impression is slightly melancholic. The villages are peaceful, some of them very attractive, demonstrating signs of wealth and civic pride, but they lack the outward gaiety of the Rheingau villages. The Rhine panorama from Nackenheim to Nierstein is, in style, more like a beautiful elegy than a stirring bacchanale — no wonder our Victorian ancestors found it picturesque, as their sketches and tour accounts show. There are plenty of comfortable weinstuben here, although it is a waste of time looking for de luxe or even smart hotels or restaurants.

After World War II, this district was under French occupation and, on the whole, it made a less rapid recovery than the Rheingau or Wiesbaden, which were occupied by the American forces. Now, however, it has sprung ahead and the town of Mainz shows signs of quite astonishing and modern development, which is almost incongruous alongside the great Cathedral and what was left after the bombing of the innumerable old-fashioned streets. The centre of Mainz was badly damaged and it must have fired the planners with sufficient courage to convert the town centre into a pedestrian precinct, where no cars are permitted. This part of

Mainz is admirably laid out.

Mainz has an impressive history, starting in Roman times. It has proud traditions, having been the seat of the Elector Archbishops. As the birthplace of Johannes Gutenberg, who evolved movable type, it is the cradle of printing. The events of its history may be studied in its splendid museums. Along the impressive Rhine waterfront, though unfortunately separated from the river itself by an eight-lane road and the ramparts of a bridge, is the former seat of government and the Elector's palace. These buildings are now partly used as the 'Landtag' (Land Parliament) — the seat of local government. On the river is a very ambitious piece of development: a modern town hall has just been finished, standing on a platform, raised on stilts to first floor level, at right angles to the River. It is a fine concept in bronze and marble. Another individual adjoining building is the Rheingold Hall, the prime object of which is to accommodate the crowds who attend the great fancy dress balls that take place at carnival time. Next door is a modern hotel, completing a luxurious meeting and conference centre, all high enough to be out of reach of the occasional severe floods when the Rhine overflows its banks.

Alzey is a largish, fairly modern town in the heart of the Rheinhessen wine district, with a modern approach to town planning, but Worms ranks high as a place of history and tradition. It is of enormous significance in history, although space cannot permit an account of its traditions here, except very briefly. It was in Worms, of course, that Martin Luther was denounced for heresy. Here too, one of the oldest, most established and influential Jewish communities in Germany flourished from the eleventh century. Its standing was only shattered in the Nazi era of the 1930s and 1940s. But Worms holds a unique position because of its Church of Our Lady or Liebfrauenkirche, or rather because of the vineyard, which is literally in the enclosure in front of the — rather plain and dull — church.

This is the Liebfrauenstift vineyard and very picturesque it looks, both in pictures and when it is viewed from a little distance away. When one gets nearer, it is perhaps just a vineyard — but certainly the vineyard that gave the most famous German wine name to the drinking public — Liebfraumilch.

There are many discussions about the origin of this term, which is mentioned as early 1703. Some people think it derives from the word 'minch' meaning 'monk', but there are other researchers who still think that the word 'milch' or milk simply does mean 'milk', and that the wines produced in the vineyard of the Church of Our Lady were, indeed, 'Our Lady's Milk',

The Liebfrauenkirche at Worms, whose vineyard gave its name to Liebfraumilch

because they were so good. Today, of course, the term 'Liebfraumilch' means something different (see p 44) but the wines of the Liebfrauenstift, although they perhaps never attain the top levels, are still sold and worth trying.

The Liebfrauenstift vineyard belongs to several owners today, of which Langenbach is perhaps the most important. But, from this area that is really the size of a large allotment, only a small amount of wine is made each year — not much more than a hundred thousand litres. They can, in the right year, be quite good — but no more; and they have a slightly earthy character that is all right with certain foods but will show to little advantage beside the more refined wines of the area.

No one visiting the Rheinhessen must skip Worms — even for a few minutes' stop. Even if you cannot go into the Liebfrauenstift enclosure, it is possible to look through the gate and see the vineyard — so as to say afterwards that you have seen it. Remember though that the Liebfraumilch wines and their origin are nowadays much more widely defined (see p 44 for further explanation).

The large Rheinhessen plain is very fertile, with medium to heavy soil, except actually on the river banks. Market gardens abound. Particularly in Nackenheim and Bodenheim, red sandstone and slate are abundantly in evidence; the red colour is obvious even to the tourist in a hurry.

Out of about 200 specified communities in Rheinhessen, nearly 170 are primarily devoted to wine growing. There is an increase in the activity of the co-operatives. Whereas certain small-scale growers have cultivated a large variety of grapes, following their own methods of vinification, a good part of production has now been absorbed by the co-operatives. The quality estates are of a somewhat more bourgeois type than those in the Rheingau, but they all nowadays follow up to date methods of vinification. South of Oppenheim, villages such as Alsheim and Mittenheim have pioneered experiments with new crossings of grapes. The soil here is fertile and favours such enterprise.

It is largely the Rheinhessen which is responsible for the success of the Siegerrebe and Scheurebe grapes and their successors on the market today. The majority of grapes in the Rheinhessen are Müller-Thurgau, then comes the Sylvaner; the Riesling is now far behind. The Portugieser and a small amount of Pinot Noir are planted near Ingelheim, which has gained repute as one of the best red wine districts in Germany. In a good year, the advantages of the Müller-Thurgau and the Sylvaner are overwhelming. With the bulk yield and the early ripening, these grape varieties have the advantage over the Riesling, however much lovers of this noble grape may wish otherwise.

The fine wine centres in the Rheinhessen are Bodenheim, Nackenheim and Nierstein, with Oppenheim and Dienheim following. The red soil enables the grapes to grow to perfection, producing wines that are stayers, with great character, showing the typical assertive scent and full flavour of the matured fruit. Nierstein has been a well known — and easy to pronounce — German wine name for some time on export markets. Its wines range from those of everyday quality to those of top character. The new Wine Law (see Chapter 4) largely continues to enable many villages and vineyards to benefit from the cover name of 'Nierstein', now Bereich Nierstein — their styles, as well as the soils of their vineyards, are similar. It is worth noting that, in contrast to this, the production of villages from the south or west has now, according to the 1971 Law, received new names, previously unknown outside their locality. For example, Wonnegau, south of Nierstein, is a district making good wines, previously differently marketed. But time will tell if this confusion will merit a further adjustment of the regulations.

In general, the wines of Nierstein and its neighbouring vineyards are good, fruity, not too light in character and easy to drink. Back from the Rhine, in small villages such as Harxheim, Mettenheim, Westhofen, Osthofen and Bechtheim, wines of weight and character are made; these, when in the hands of determined and courageous growers, are capable of reaching a high level of quality, achieving an almost voluptuous and harmonious style.

Oppenheim, in addition to its vineyards, is the seat of a well-known Wine Institute which has done good work in raising the standard of viticulture and vinification. The Staatsweingut for Hessen, at one time an important owner of vineyards, has, (it is hoped only temporarily), closed.

Although Rheinhessen is not, perhaps, as obviously beautiful or spectacular as some of the wine regions, its wines are popular everywhere and its easy accessibility from Mainz and Wiesbaden makes it a profitable excursion. All along the roads small inns and eating places make it enjoyable for the tourist to stop — and the wines will make an immediate appeal.

Rheinpfalz

This is a wine region of great charm, with picture-postcard villages clustering on the sides of hills, several of which are crowned by ruined castles. It was in one of these castles, in fact, that Richard Coeur de Lion, King Richard I of England, was imprisoned in 1194 after he had been captured when returning from a Crusade; his friend and court musician, Blondel, travelled far and wide searching for his master. One day, singing beneath the walls of one of the castles near Neustadt (Trifels, above Annweiler), Blondel heard Richard's voice giving back the refrain and, having thus found out where the King was, the minstrel returned to England and arranged for the monarch's ransom to be paid.

The name 'Palatinate', which is the English version of 'Pfalz', comes from the Latin word 'palatium', meaning a palace or seat of government where the Roman Governor stayed. The region has been of considerable importance since Roman times. The German word 'palast' which derived from 'palatium' eventually became Pfalz; then it was applied to the country around it. The 'Rhein' in Rheinpfalz, the Rhenish Palatinate, was added as a further geographical definition.

The local ruler or Elector was a powerful person, as, at one time, the area was much more extensive and included the fine university city of Heidelberg. In the seventeenth century the Elector of the time, Carl, married the Princess Elizabeth, daughter of James I of England, who was so beautiful and so attractive that she was known as 'the Queen of Hearts'; however, when Elector Carl and his lovely wife were offered the crown of Bohemia in 1620 they left the Palatinate and went to Prague where, unfortunately, they were driven out by the Austrians and fled into exile at The Hague when the snows melted — hence Elizabeth's other nickname, 'the Winter Queen'. One of Elizabeth's sons was the warrior prince popularly known as 'Rupert of the Rhine'.

The Rheinpfalz, as it is usually termed in Germany, begins

almost immediately south of the gently undulating plains of Rheinhessen. The 80 kilometres of vineyards begin above Grunstadt and stretch below the ridge of the Haardt mountains, almost straight southwards to the French frontier. Indeed, in terms of formation, the Pfalz continues into France as what has become the Alsace wine area.

The Rheinpfalz is easy of access from several of the main autoroutes: those of Frankfurt/Mannheim; Koblenz/Bingen/Ludwigshaven/Speyer; and Paris/Saarbrucken/Kaiserslautern/Frankenthal. The rail centre is Mannheim. Frankfurt is the airport that immediately serves the region. Hotels actually in the Rheinpfalz are no longer small and unpretentious, but remain very comfortable, and visitors are always happily aware that they are essentially in the country, usually within easy walking distance of fields and vineyards. There are hundreds of weinstuben in all the villages and restaurants of interest in all the towns. The people are outgoing and jolly in character, the girls pretty and buxom, the men in general exuberant about enjoying themselves — but, as a grandson of this blessed district, I may be prejudiced in its favour!

The vineyard region today is only about eight to ten kilometres in width, running along the east of the Haardt Mountains, which provide protection against the harsh winds; they also give shelter against any fierce daytime heat and the humidity of the Rhine plain contributes to a superbly mild, warm climate. In former times, it was customary to speak of the areas of the Upper, Middle and Lower Haardt. Today, however, according to the new nomenclature, the region consists of the Mittelhaardt-Deutsche Weinstrasse (German Wine Route), which runs from the north down as far as Neustadt, plus the Südliche Weinstrasse (Southern Wine Route) which starts at Neustadt and goes down to the French frontier. The soil is quite variable, with sandstone predominating in the hills, plus chalk, granite, porphyry and slate in patches throughout the district, thereby resulting in many different types of wine being made even within the same small parish. A great deal of wine is produced overall and must today account for about thirty per cent of total German wine production.

Fifty per cent of the white wine grapes are Müller-Thurgau and Sylvaner, with Riesling accounting for only about twenty-five per cent. The Scheurebe, Morio Muskat and Kerner varieties are becoming popular. About ten per cent of the acreage under vines is planted with the red Portugieser, which, near Bad Dürkheim, makes a pleasant red wine. Of all the producers, about two-thirds of these are in the category 'mixed agricultural', including vines, with about one-third devoting themselves entirely to making wine; these, together with the old-established estates, which follow traditional methods, mostly undertake distribution of the wines themselves, but about a quarter of the production is handled by the co-operatives and the remainder is sold to the wine trade by the producers.

The wines vary in style and quality. The Riesling comes into its own in the Mittelhaardt, where it produces wines of great backbone, character and fruit. The wines of the Mittelhaardt are, on the whole, almost voluptuous, not too heavy, with a great aroma of the grape plus a hint of earthiness; they are great stayers, enjoying long lives when well made in the right year. If a comparison has to be made, it can be said they perhaps lack the somewhat stern structure of the great Rheingau wines. In an ordinary year, the slight earthiness of Rheinpfalz wines is an attractive taste base on which the aroma of the locality develops to full advantage. But Mittelhaardt wines of a good year possess considerable style and elegance, with great strength of body; they are very well rounded and, where they lack a certain type of fruit acidity, it has the effect of making them appear slightly sweeter than Rheingau wines. The wine makers have become artists in cultivating the highly scented grapes Scheurebe, Siegerrebe, Traminer, and the Auslesen, Beerenauslesen and Trockenbeerenauslesen are great drinking experiences, even if somewhat overwhelming. Another asset of Rheinpfalz wines that will delight the visitor is that the lower and medium priced wines are robust enough to partner many foods, including some of the informal regional specialities.

Although space does not permit this book to include accounts of the great wine makers of the German wine regions, it is important to remember that, in the Rheinpfalz, the 'three Bs' are outstanding, as producers of the very finest wines of the area: these growers are Bassermann-Jordan, von Buhl and Dr Bürklin-Wolf. Each makes wines of distinctive style and, although none of the finest are in the cheap range, it is well worth trying a bottle or half bottle while on the spot as a special treat. Von Buhl and Bassermann-Jordan have their head-quarters at Deidesheim, Dr Bürklin-Wolf is at Wachenheim; the name 'Bürklin' is recorded as early as 1579 as owning vineyards. The establishment thoughtfully bottles many of its Beerenauslesen and Trockenbeerenauslesen in half bottle sizes, so that it is possible to sip a little of an outstanding wine to register a memorable experience on the spot. These Pfalz wines rightly claim their place among the 'greats' of Germany and are admired for their superb harmony and balance.

The Deutsche Weinstrasse is a delightful route to follow.

Half-timbered house at Kallstadt

Grunstadt, in the north, has an attractive old church and houses and, a little further on, Kallstadt is the northern bastion of the classic Rheinpfalz wines, which, up to this point tend to be pleasant but without great distinction. In Kallstadt, they start to show the real Pfalz style — they are full, almost rich, with marked fruit, although they are never harsh or unbalanced.

Bad Dürkheim is an ideal centre for tourism and studying wine. It is, as its name implies, a spa, with attractive parks and gardens, a casino, old churches and good hotels. Almost within walking distance is the old town of Wachenheim, with the ruined castle of Wachtenburg. Bad Dürkheim annually holds an enormous wine fair in September, called the Sausage Market, at which vast quantities of different types of sausages provide 'blotting paper' for the wines available for sampling. The ten days of this festival are, inevitably, very noisy and the town is packed — so avoid it then if you want quiet. Many thirsty souls are packed into the restaurant there that is actually built inside a gigantic cask, which towers above the nearby houses; others are accommodated in tents and marquees. The Pfalzers enjoy taking advantage of any excuse for a celebration and, in addition to the vintage festivals in many towns, there is an asparagus festival at Weisenheim, a radish festival at Schifferstadt, and a 'brezel' (pretzel) festival at Speyer! There are also many festivals that welcome the advent of spring, including the auction of a ram at Deidesheim on the Tuesday after Whitsun. Anyone who can see something of such festivals, with the colourful local costumes, lively songs and dances, will certainy agree that the purpose of wine is to 'make glad the heart of man'!

Wachenheim is so attractive that time should, if possible, be allocated to a stop to explore it. Two kilometres further south, the wines of Forst are not unlike those of Wachenheim, although those who try the wines of the Forster Jesuitengarten (Garden of the Jesuits) may agree that here some of the strength and sturdiness of Wachenheim has been replaced by a more stylish elegance.

Deidesheim, three kilometres further south, is a larger place, with an attractive market square, town hall and fountain and many old houses, plus a very pleasant old hostelry, the Kanne (Can). Until recently, largely in the medium priced range of wines, it was the name of Deidesheim that made the wines of this region known throughout the world — although one supposes that most non-Germans would have found it easier to pronounce the name of Forst. The great wines of Deidesheim may be put on the same level as those of Wachenheim and Forst and they often achieve even greater harmony and balance.

Below Deidesheim, to the east, Ruppertsberg and, to the west, Königsbach introduce the more southern style of Rheinpfalz wines: the powerful fruitiness and full-bodied character is less pronounced and, in good years, there is an upsurge of delightful floweriness and bouquet, with great style and delicacy.

A little further to the south, the villages of Mussbach and Gimmeldingen independently produce wines that are most agreeable and somewhat light. They strictly belong to the Neustadt area. They are charming huddles of attractive little houses, some of which have been turned into pleasant country restaurants and weinstuben, where it is easy to lose count of time as one wanders about, combining sightseeing with tasting, away from contemporary pressures. Neustadt itself is a busy town, with some light industry, delightful pedestrian shopping precincts, and a curious church shared between Catholics and Protestants. It is very much a wine centre: there is a wine training college here, also the editorial offices of several wine journals and much manufacture of wine-making equipment. The many vineyards do not, however, produce quite the same quality of wine as the more northern stretch of vineyards up to Bad Dürkheim.

Still further south, around Maikammer and Edenkoben, there is a lot of wine made, pleasant, even good, but with perhaps no outstandingly high quality. Edenkoben, with its remnants of a Cistercian monastery, and the old town walls of Landau, make it worth while for the traveller to stop at both places en route. Further on, near Schweigen, there is the mighty Weintor, or 'Wine Gate', on the crest of a rise, overlooking France. The whole of this region is perfect for leisurely exploration and, at night, the gabled houses of the villages, with their cobbled streets and squares, look like the setting for some enchanting operetta.

A detour from the main route south through the Rheinpfalz should certainly be made for a visit to Speyer. Travellers with enough time should of course also see Heidelberg, but Speyer has particular claims on the attention of the lover of wine. Like Worms, Speyer was a Roman settlement and later became a bishopric. The Cathedral — an impressive edifice from the outside, but rather dull and with somewhat banal nineteenth century frescoes inside — was founded in 1030. Many of the German Emperors are buried at Speyer. The Cathedral has played a part in British history, too: it was while the then Prince of Wales, later Edward VII of England, was being shown round Speyer Cathedral, that he was able to see for the first time his bride to be, the then Princess Alexandra of Denmark.

Opposite the Cathedral, the Historisches Museum der Pfalz is worth seeing anyway, but it also houses an important Wine Museum; here visitors may inspect implements used in vine cultivation since Roman times and old presses, as well as a fine collection of drinking vessels and casks and cask heads. These were traditionally decorated to commemorate events of special historic or social significance, such as the winters when the River Rhine was frozen over. The most famous exhibit, however, is an amphora dating from the third century AD, which contains a liquid that scientists have been able to testify is still recognisable as wine! Cloudy and strange as it looks, it is probably the oldest sample of wine in the world.

Franken

The wine region of Franken, usually known to us as Franconia, is not large in size, but it produces wines of classic quality and well deserves a visit. The valley of the River Main, in which it lies, is very pleasant, even if not as impressive as the Rhine Gorge or the lovely Mosel. And although the scenery is not as dramatic as the steeply terraced slopes of some of the German wine river valleys, the banks of the Main provide a panorama of constantly varied scenery.

Politically, the Main has for long been of considerable importance. True, it is the River Rhine that, historically, has formed a natural frontier for Germany and, even today, acts in this way in the south of the Federal Republic. But the River Main has always been regarded as the great dividing line between north and south Germany, separating the two main regions which, in the past, have contended for supreme power — Prussia in the north versus south Germany and its allies. It is the Main that has always been considered the principal division.

Franconia is easy of access by the Frankfurt/Würzburg/Nürnberg autobahn and the Kassel/Würzburg/Stuttgart autobahn, which intersect in Würzburg. Rail connections are good between Frankfurt and Würzburg and the Frankfurt airport is about an hour's drive from Würzburg.

The climate, while still temperate, tends to be more 'continental' than that of any other German wine area, the temperature, in both summer and winter, tending to rise and fall to a greater extent.

The soil, too, varies considerably: it is nowhere too heavy for quality wine production and consists partly of sediment, partly of sandstone.

The vines grown are largely Müller-Thurgau, which accounts for about fifty per cent today, with the Sylvaner contributing about one-third of the whole. The Riesling accounts for a mere ten per cent and new crossbreeds, such as Scheurebe, Kerner and Bacchus, together with others still at the experimental stage, make up the remainder. Viticulturalists are searching for a comparatively early maturing grape, to suit a region where frosts in late spring and early autumn are not uncommon.

Throughout the Middle Ages, Franconia was one of the largest wine-producing areas of all Germany. There is evidence of viticulture dating from the eighth century and the various monasteries and religious houses, as well as the great estates of the feudal nobility, encouraged the making of wine. The devastation of the whole region in the Thirty Years' War, 1618-1648, started a decline which unfortunately continues, much of the area that was formerly under vines being given up to farming, so that essential food crops have been steadily taking over. Such vineyards as survived or have developed today are on the southern slopes of the hills, where the vine can flourish in spite of the unfavourable climate.

The wines have established themselves as quite different in character from all others in Germany: to say that they are 'steely' in character is perhaps rather sweeping, but they certainly remind the drinker of the stony soil from which they come. They possess a dry, fruity style, but lack the immediate appeal — which is sometimes almost a feminine allure — of the wines that come from the Mosel and the Nahe.

The term 'Steinwein' is often used to signify Franconian wines — again, perhaps because of their steely, stony character. But the term 'Steinwein' should only be used in reference to the wines actually from the Stein site at Würzburg, even though many people still use the word 'Stein' rather loosely. The term has nothing to do with the mug-like drinking vessel called a 'Stein', although Franconian wines are easy to recognise, because they are all bottled in the 'Bocksbeutel', a flagon-like dark green bottle. This is interesting in itself, for it is a survival from the time when wineskins had to be used for transporting small quantities of wine about; the Bocksbeutel is in fact a glass version of the scrotum of a goat, which was used in medieval times.

A small quantity of red wine is also made in Franconia, of which that of Iphofen is perhaps the best-known; although it seldom achieves more than an agreeable style, it is certainly worth while trying when you are in the region.

Franconia is divided into three districts: to the west, there is the Main Viereck (Main rectangle), which in fact looks more like a flat-topped 'U'; this is based on the main configurations of the Main Valley. This 'U' has Aschaffenburg at one corner and finishes just short of Gemünden. Here, the Main Dreieck (Main triangle) starts, with Würzburg at the southern point of the triangle, Schweinfurt, further up the Main, as its eastern boundary. The third region is Steigerwald, which extends around Kitzingen.

The Michelin Green Guide 'Germany' suggests a 98km tour of the Main Valley vineyards, via Soomerhausen, Ochsenfurt, Frickenhausen, Marktbreit, Sulzfeld, Kitzingen, Iphofen, Wiesentheid, Prichenstadt and Dettelbach, which takes four to five hours if stops are made to look around. A guidebook is certainly essential for any visitor to Würzburg and its surroundings to enjoy to the full this attractive, comparatively little-known area. Other excursions from Würzburg might include one on the road B27 south-west to Tauberbischofsheim, on the River Tauber, which is a tributary of the Main. The well-named Romantische Strasse (Romantic Road), which starts on the B290 and goes through Weikersheim to Rothenburg, leads the traveller through beautiful scenery and Rothenburg is a picture-postcard seventeenth century town. It is then possible to return on the B25 and B13, via Offenheim, Ochsenfurt and Sommerhausen.

Another excursion to the south-east from Würzburg might include the wine villages of Randersacker, Sommerhausen and Marktbreit, where the Main turns sharply north. The wine road goes to Kitzingen, which should be seen for its Renaissance town hall, the parish church and remains of the old town walls, then northwards to Sommerach, Volkach and Eschendorf, to Wipfeld, a little short of Schweinfurth. Southeast of Kitzingen, one can go to Iphofen on the B8 then, northwards on the B286, continue past Castell, with its attractive park and church, and take the B22 to Bamberg, a

particularly charming Baroque town astride the River Regnitz.
Bamberg is well worth a stop, especially to see the
Karolingen Platz, bounded on one side by the Cathedral and
on another by the Renaissance Residenz. On the other two sides
it is bounded by the Neue Residenz, built in the eighteenth
century by the Bishop Lothar-Franz von Schönborn — whose
family are still esteemed makers of wine. Beautiful though this
— and indeed all Bamberg — is, it is overshadowed by the
work of a nephew of Lothar-Franz and another, later, von
Schönborn, who finished the wonderful Residenz at Würzburg.
There are so many treasures here, and indeed, delightful places
to taste wine, that time must be allowed for a leisurely pause.

Of special interest to British travellers, Coburg and Rosenau,
where Albert, Prince Consort, was born, are near enough for
excursions to be made. Bayreuth, for Wagnerians, is not too
far, either.

Würzburg, however, is the focal point of Franconia. It is a
stately, handsome town, with friendly, hospitable inhabitants.
The Residenz, built in 1720 and finished in 1744, is one of the
largest Baroque palaces in the whole of Germany. The
churches and gardens of this picturesque town merit lengthy
exploration as well. The great sculptor, Tilman
Riemenschneider (1460-1531) lived for most of his life in
Würzburg and enriched it with many of his works.

But Würzburg has some remarkable wine establishments as
well as art treasures. The Bayerische Landesanstalt für Wein-
und Gartenbau (Bavarian Institute for Viticulture and
Horticulture) owns more than one hundred hectares of
vineyards, with holdings extending throughout the main wine-
growing region of this area. The Staatsweingut Hofkellerei (the
Court Cellar) which it also owns, is a showplace of a wine cellar
and tasting room, right underneath the Residenz; this, like
other properties, was relinquished to the Bavarian Government
by the former Bishops and Dukes of Franconia at the end of the
Napoleonic wars in the early nineteenth century.

Then there is the Juliusspital (Julius Hospice), named for
Julius Echter von Mespelbrunn, who founded it in the latter
part of the sixteenth century. This is endowed with vineyards
bequeathed with money or gifts of land so that, today, it is an
establishment owning perhaps the greatest amount of land
under vines in an individual holding of all Germany. But the
oldest of all the Würzburg foundations is that of the
Bürgerspital zum Heiligen Geist (The Citizens' Hospital of the
Holy Spirit), which was established by Johann von Steren in
1319. Today, there are 120 old men living here, the average
age being 82! This says much for the medieval wine ration that
inhabitants of the Bürgerspital were allowed — half a litre a

day. Each one of these establishments may be seen and wines tasted in the bars maintained by them for the benefit of tourists — and for the upkeep of the foundations.

There are other Franconian estates, but the co-operatives also play a great part in the maintenance of the wine traditions of this proud region.

Baden — Württemberg

The former kingdom of Württemberg and the Grand Duchy of Baden were united in 1945. The two regions are delightful — it will be remembered how many of our ancestors went to the various spas there and explored the countryside. There is every type of scenic beauty: steep river banks, fortresses, towers, terraced vineyards and lonely, volcanic crags, undulating hills, dark forests, the snow-capped Alps in the background on a clear day, and many things of interest to explore in the towns. There is an unrivalled concentration of good hotels and excellent restaurants — and the inhabitants drink more wine per head than anywhere else in Germany! The Baden people are amusing and charming, with lighthearted, easy ways; Württembergers have a reputation for stubbornness, a capacity for hard work and a dry sense of humour.

WÜRTTEMBERG

Württemberg, like Franconia, used to be one of the main wine areas of Germany before the Thirty Years' War, from which it has never really recovered. In the nineteenth century strenuous efforts were made to restore the production area, but the results were disappointing. Today attempts are being made to reform all this but, as the per capita consumption is so high, Württemberg wines are seldom seen on export markets — all the more reason for trying as many as possible while in the region.

The climate is changeable, the region protected by the Swabian Alps to the north-east and the Schwarzwald (Black Forest) to the west. The area under vines has indeed increased since 1950, but is still only about one-fifth what it was at the outbreak of the Thirty Years' War in 1618. the soil varies a great deal; there is both loess and loam, changing from a rich, heavy, almost clay-like consistency to more meagre formations.

There are many different grape varieties cultivated here. The most widely planted is the Trollinger, with its dark blue skin. It makes a red wine which is a sturdy, pleasant drink, found nowhere else in Germany. The fruit acidity of this variety makes it popular in a mild warm climate. The Trollinger probably originated in the southern Tirol, where it is still popular and whence its name may derive. The Pinot Noir, Portugieser and a few other black grapes are also cultivated and, in the 7,500 hectares of vineyards, only fifty per cent is planted with white grapes, making white wine. The Riesling is the most important of these, with the Sylvaner, Müller-Thurgau and some of the new crossings also contributing.

In Württemberg, Heilbronn is a pretty town, well worth seeing, and so is nearby Bad Wimpfen with remnants of the Kaiser's Castle; also Weinsberg, a ruined castle, and Neckarsulm with its Baroque church and museum of the motorcycle. Bad Mergentheim is an attractive spa, with a castle formerly belonging to the Teutonic Knights' order. Maulbronn, west of Heilbronn, has one of the oldest Cistercian abbeys in Germany. Stuttgart itself, perhaps rather too modern for the traveller in search of the picturesque, is nevertheless attractively laid out and very much a wine town — vines are actually grown within 250 yards of the central railway station! The Schillerplatz, in the heart of the old town, has the statue of the great poet, Schiller, who was born in nearby Marbach and spent his youth here, and, in the Altes Schloss (the Old Castle) there is the regional museum and the former ducal cellars, which are still in use. All along the nearby valley of the River Neckar the vineyards make the landscape full of charm and interest.

BADEN

Baden has the third largest area under vines in all Germany, but, even though it has doubled in size since 1950, it is still far from what it was a century ago. Climatically, it is ideal for wine growing — more so than Württemberg. It is more protected and has several sites that are really fine. The soil varies enormously, from rich to chalky, with sandstone and a rough sprinkling of volcanic elements.

Probably the best-known wine of all comes from the Kaiserstuhl, which is a volcanic stump of a hill that rises above the Rhine plain north-west of Freiburg. Here, in the right weather conditions, the Kaiserstuhl vineyards produce many powerful, weighty wines, from the Ruländer, Gewürztraminer and other grapes — and even from the black grape, the Pinot Noir. Further south, between Basel and Freiburg, in the Markgräfler region, a grape is still cultivated which, in the past, was grown virtually everywhere in Germany — the Gutedel. This, because of its low acidity, can even be used as a table grape. The wine it makes is mild, elegant and drinks well, but it should be consumed young because it tires as it gets old. There are many sub-species of the Gutedel, some of them varying slightly as to the degree of reddish skin colour, and the wine made by certain of these can have a slight Muscat flavour.

Wines from the surroundings of the Bodensee (Lake Constance) are interesting, because the vineyards are cultivated at an altitude of up to 1200 feet above sea level. They have great style, but a certain pronounced fruit acidity because of this.

Another popular region for good wines is the Ortenau: this, on the plain and in the valleys of the Schwarzerwald between Baden-Baden and Offenburg, makes wines that enjoy considerable reputations in the locality. In the region between Freiburg and Offenburg, which is known as the Breisgau, red wines are made and also whites from the Ruländer and Traminer grapes, but these rarely attain the quality levels of those made in the nearby Kaiserstuhl region.

Vineyards in Baden-Württemberg used in the past to be part of the mixed agricultural holdings of small farmers, but slowly co-operatives have begun to achieve marked results. There are also some big estates. The great modern establishment, the Zentralkellerei, of the co-operative in Breisach, is worth seeing.

TWO SPECIALITIES

Württemberg and, to a certain extent, Baden are the homeland of German pink wine, or rosé. There are two kinds: one is made simply by pressing red or black grapes immediately after picking, so that the must or unfermented juice absorbs just sufficient of the pigment in the grapeskins to tint the wine a pleasant rosy colour. Such wines have a pleasing touch of astringency and tannin on the palate.

The other method involves mixing both red (black) and white grapes at the time of the vintage and fermenting them together. The resulting wine has an intriguing taste, combining the style of the white grapes with that of the red. This wine is locally known as 'Schillerwein', derived either from the poet Schiller or from the German verb schillern, which means 'to shimmer, glitter' which it certainly does when sampled on a sunny day in a sympathetic weinstube. Production of this Schillerwein, or Rotling, is permitted only in Württemberg and, it should be stressed, the mixture of red and white grapes has to be made prior to the start of the process of fermentation, as the blending of red and white wines to make a subsequent pink is not allowed by German law.

A Baden speciality is 'Weissherbst'; this term means 'white picked'. It signifies that the wine has been made from a blue-skinned grape, like the Spätburgunder, or Pinot Noir. Instead of letting the fermenting must acquire the colour of the grapeskins by allowing them to remain in it so as to impart their tint, the grapes are pressed and treated as if they were white, with the skins removed. The wine is essentially white too, very delicate and capable of attaining considerable quality in the right conditions.

Visiting in the wine regions

Transport throughout Germany is good, but of course the ideal for the visitor is to have a car. Even if you do not take your own, it may be worth hiring one for a few days, so as to get the maximum benefit from a series of vineyard visits, although bear in mind that traffic controls are strict so, unless you are really sure of yourself as a driver on the continent and also can be certain that you are not likely to enjoy German wines too much on a day's outing, it is advisable to see whether you can hire a driver to take you around. The maps that you will find helpful are recommended in Appendix 3.

A very pleasant way of seeing a great many famous vineyards in a short time is to take one of the river cruises. The steamers call at a number of points on both the Mosel and the Rhine and, in the high season, services are frequent. You can certainly drink and have snacks on these boats and, often, full-scale meals too. Mosel cruises can be leisurely, because of the sharp bends in the river; Rhine cruises are faster and cover more ground. Even if your visit to Germany is short, you may still be able to see something of the well-known vineyards by looking out of the train window — the luxury expresses pass along both banks of both the Rhine and through the Rhine Gorge and, if you can follow your journey on one of the maps that indicate the panoramas along the banks, you will at least be able to register what the vineyards look like.

Shops and tourist information centres are usually open throughout the week and, unlike those in some other countries, do not close on Mondays; however, in the cities Saturday afternoon tends to be a time when all business establishments and some shops are shut.

TASTING

In general, very few of the big estates or even the co-operatives are geared to offer tastings to the visiting public, unless it has been possible to arrange this beforehand, but the 'strauss-wirtschaft' is a licensed eating-place that will sell the owner's wine for a limited period and also any local specialities, such as sausages and cheeses. A green bush — the 'strauss' — is hoisted outside the door, thereby indicating that the establishment is open for trade, an interesting reminder of the green 'bush' that used to be hoisted outside English taverns to signal the arrival of the new wine of the season, and which gave rise to the saying 'Good wine needs no bush'.

If you are able to have a tasting arranged for you, you may or may not find spittoons with the range of wine set out along a tasting table, with several glasses so that you are able to compare wine with wine. Sometimes, out of misplaced courtesy, a wine establishment will offer glasses that are both grand in style, such as the 'Römer' (see p 31) and very large, but you can usually get a more modest type of glass if you ask.

British tourists should be reminded that it is important to shake hands with everybody, both when you arrive and when you leave. It is conventional for everyone to do so, therefore the visitor should be ready to offer his or her hand to all.

Tipping is somewhat of a problem. Obviously, you do not tip an important executive of a firm and, even lower down the scale, to offer a tip may be considered an insult, unless of course it is patent that some form of monetary thanks is expected. A small sum may be given to anyone who has gone to extra trouble for the visitor — such as to a junior cellarman, who has been getting samples out of a cask, balancing precariously on ladders, but, in general, it is advisable to be careful about offering money, although thanks should naturally be expressed.

Even if you don't speak any German, remember that it is a mark of politeness to address people by their titles — that is, the office that they hold: in descending order, there may be the Herr Direktor, the Prokurist (a senior executive who is entitled to sign contracts), the Kellermeister (cellarmaster), or frequently Kufermeister (cooper, although not someone who works in a cooperage assembling casks (a Holzküfer), but possibly the supervisor of the vats and what is in them, as well as any technical equipment), and — rather on his own — the Rentmeister, who is the senior bailiff who runs the estate. Each one of these gets a prefatory 'Herr' to his title if you are being courteous and it does save trying to remember someone's actual name if you can be sure of their official status.

It should go without saying that, if an appointment has been made for you to see a person or visit an establishment, you should be punctual. If you are delayed, try to get someone to telephone on your behalf — most people will find you somebody who speaks English if they cannot themselves help you, and of course an hotel or a large garage will certainly have somebody who can translate and make a telephone call on your behalf.

As far as the great estates are concerned, it is worth taking some trouble if you are fortunate enough to be introduced and can go and taste there. Remember that these great estates deal almost exclusively with brokers and the trade; they are not selling a proprietary article and they employ few staff. Owners are always delighted and flattered to hear pleasant comments on their wines, but they seldom have the facilities, labour, or time to show visitors around and to open bottles to show samples, even if they would like to. All samples and tastings have to be prepared, the wines must be at the right temperature, the sample room properly arranged, and there must be someone in authority who can answer questions. Very few estates are equipped for that but even if you can't visit them, remember that most do show wines at the various wine fairs, where they sell wine by the glass and bottle (see p 95). Sparkling wine manufacturers are more geared to publicity and are able to receive visitors (see pp 36-7).

Once in the tasting room, certain elementary rules apply to all tastings. There must be no distracting smells, smoke, scent, after-shave lotions — or children. Nosing and tasting require absolute concentration and the serious taster is deaf and blind. He can't hear you when you talk unless he interrupts his tasting, thereby causing waste of time and irritation.

As a good taster, you will first look at the wine and compare its colour with that of the others. See whether it is bright, crystal clear, if it has thrown a sediment or if it produces those delightful small bubbles which you find mostly in the youthful Mosels. Raise the glass to your nose and sniff the bouquet. Put the glass to your mouth and take a sip, letting it roll around your tongue. If you drink without spitting out the wine, it will quickly saturate your palate to such an extent that, after five or six samples you will be unable to make any more fine distinctions. (The fact that you will also get drunk is only a secondary consideration.) If, in such tasting rooms, you want to spit (and you should) there are usually spittoons on the floor or, if you are in a cellar, you use the cellar floor. It does not take much practice to become competent.

To taste properly, suck a little air through the wine as it enters your mouth and don't hesitate to make a noise when you roll the wine around your tongue. There is a good reason for this: by its very nature and physiology, the tongue can't taste anything but sweet, sour, bitter and salt. But pulling a sip of wine into the mouth in this way gets its aroma right to the back of the nose, which acts as the great indicator and analyst. This is why, when you have a cold, you cannot taste either wine or food: the smell system which is based in the nose is out of order. For this reason you should allow the back of your nose to share in tasting.

It is important to compare different wines with each other, because this is the easiest and best method of analysing taste. There may be a wine which, to you, stands out. Compare it with all the others and try to remember it, since it is one you like. This does not necessarily mean that the wine is better, but

Statuette from Öhringen, Württemberg, 1667; the vat can be used as a drinking vessel

it is the wine that is, so to speak, on your wavelength and you will usually find you will always prefer that style.

To analyse a wine properly, you and your palate must be completely fresh and rested, so the best time for tasting is in the morning, between 10 am and 11.30 am, as far as I am concerned. When the palate gets tired and you feel thirsty, any wine becomes more acceptable than would normally be the case.

On a tasting tour, the ideal lunch must be somewhat dull, possibly even just boiled beef and carrots. More spicy fare, certain fruit that is very acid, onions and, of course, curry will put the palate out of action. Beware of the man who says he always tastes his wine at night reasoning that, after all, this is the time when you are supposed to drink it! When a brewery buyer once boasted of this tasting habit, his host replied suavely that, as a rich man and frequent purchaser of jewellery, the brewer therefore doubtless made his selections late at night, in a ballroom illuminated by multicoloured neon lights — for that, after all, was the right place to wear emeralds, wasn't it? The brewer gracefully acknowledged defeat and, it is said, changed his ways.

Selection of wines for dinner in the evening is a matter of personal taste. But there are general physiological rules which cannot be disregarded. Your taste and nose capacities function in a certain way which will not allow you to taste dry after sweet, or light after heavy. A clever hostess allows for this fact in the preparation of the menu and the host must do exactly the same with his wines. Start with a light, dry wine and continue or finish with a heavier and sweeter and older one. The very greatest wines like Trockenbeerenauslese are preferably drunk with fruit, such as a peach, or a not too rich sweet course, so as to balance the sweetness of the wine and allow its fruit and body to come through and speak to the drinker.

There are numerous festivals associated with wine held throughout the wine regions, but most of these do tend to be rather in the nature of promotional jamborees, rather than a means whereby a student of wine can increase his or her knowledge. In very general terms, the most usual times when the wine festivals are held tend to be during or just after the vintage — remember that it is later in the autumn in Germany than for the rest of Europe — but there are also spring and mid-summer festivals as well. The local wine information offices (See Appendix 4) or the tourist offices should be able to provide detailed particulars for visitors who may wish to see such a type of festival. For the more serious public tastings and for the big wine auctions, tickets of admission usually have to be procured in advance; the easiest way to do this is through any wine firm to which you may have arranged an introduction, although you should be prepared to pay for your ticket.

Bear in mind that all these events can, after a while, be extremely tiring, especially to the visitor whose knowledge of German is minimal. A festival may be arranged like a big exhibition, covering a large space, with people visiting the various stands merely to enjoy a series of drinks. Those in charge of wine displays will generally be most concerned to make sales, not to engage in detailed conversations about wine or conduct comparative tastings! If you take part in an organised tour, whether this is arranged by a travel agent or a wine firm, then it should certainly be possible to learn something about wine as well as enjoying a tour of the exhibition stands and, possibly, displays of dancing and singing.

Local newspapers and, of course, most hotels, will have particulars of any festivals in the vicinity and local travel agencies may be able to arrange short visits, with an interpreter, so as to help visitors to get the best from such occasions.

Sales of wine at auction tend to attract a lot of publicity — often more than they really deserve. At the beginning of the twentieth century they did serve a useful purpose but, with the growth of the wine trade, they have declined in commercial influence since World War II. Their rôle has been partly taken over by the fixed price wine fairs, such as those of Rheingau wines at Kloster Eberbach in April each year, and the May fair in Mainz for Rheingau, Rheinhessen, Rheinpfalz and Nahe wines.

In the Rheinhessen, many small estates have combined to make up groups offering wines for sale at auction, but, in spite of the phasing out of the Rheinhessen Staatsweingut (State Domaine of Hessen), their activities are still flourishing. Few sales are nowadays held in the Pfalz or Nahe regions but in Trier there are still the auctions of the Grosse Ring and Kleine Ring, which offer wines from many of the top estates; the Grosse Ring tends to have the very finest. But it has been estimated that the majority of the top growers now sell a mere fraction of their wine by auction, the balance being taken up on the open market by the regular wine trade.

Auctions can be picturesque affairs, such as the sales of rarities which take place from time to time in Wiesbaden; many people are attracted by this, because there is free tasting of the wines, both before and during the auction. The wine trade, however, are increasingly hesitant about patronising this and similar sales; this is because anyone who wishes may bid there, via a broker — and, for obvious reasons, the wine trade is reluctant to enter into direct competition with groups of private customers who, by doing business through a broker at these auctions, may get virtual 'trade rates'. The auctions can last a very long time, too, because each wine is sampled before being put up for bidding — it can be somewhat of an endurance test to sit for hours, especially if you do not have the temerity to spit the samples out, in a packed saleroom! To sell sixty wines in the German style will take from about 1 pm to 8 pm, whereas, in the salerooms of British firms such as Christie's or Sotheby's, 120 wine lots will be sold in a single hour — tasting will have been done before the sale starts.

The world record price for a single bottle of German wine sold at auction is held by the 1921 Bernkasteler Doktor Riesling Trockenbeerenauslese, of Weingut Dr H Thanisch of Bernkastel-Cues, which, in March 1978, was bought at the Wiesbaden sale for a German client for DM 7,200 (about £1,870). This, of course, was an exceptional wine anyway, but auction prices do sometimes tend to be higher than the usual market rate — the excitement and the publicity stimulate bidding.

WINE SEMINARS

A welcome addition to the wine scene in Germany has been the organisation of wine seminars, to enable serious lovers of wine to increase their knowledge and experience of the wines, under expert instruction. Most of these seminars include visits to both vineyards and firms, to historic estates and technical institutes, as well as lectures and tutored tastings of a number of wines. Most of the regions run several seminars, varying from weekend or two-day sessions to courses that last a week and combine a certain amount of sight-seeing as well as instruction. Bookings can generally be made for groups of people.

Most of these seminars, however, are held in German, so that they are not listed here. If your knowledge of the language is up to attending such courses, then the local information offices (see Appendix 4) will be able to give particulars. There are now, however, some seminars that are being held in English, so that it is worth enquiring as to what is available at different times of the year — many seminars are held outside the main holiday season for obvious reasons. Charges vary, according to whether accommodation is included.

THE GERMAN WINE ACADEMY

This is now becoming known to members of the wine trade and wine lovers from all over the world. A seven day course, in English, is held several times a year, based on Kloster Eberbach in the Rheingau and directed by Dr Hans Ambrosi, the Director of the Staatsweingut. Beginners are catered for and there is a 'postgraduate course' for former or more advanced students. For details of the sessions, apply to the various national or regional information centres or direct to Deutsches Weininstitut GmbH, Gutenbergplatz 3-5, 6500 Mainz.

Eating in Germany

The Germans are enthusiastic trenchermen and each region of the country has its own specialities. Of course, the big hotels and luxury restaurants serve food of international style as well, but the traveller will learn more about the country by eating in smaller places. These abound: if you see the sign 'Weinstube', often with an attractive wrought-iron or painted sign outside, you will know that you can get simple food, both hot and cold, as well as being able to choose from a fairly long list of wines, available by the bottle but also by the glass or carafe.

The 'open wines' — offene Weine — are those which can be ordered by the glass — 'glasweise' — the contents of which can be quite small, from about 0.10 litre, which is equivalent to a rather wee British measure, up to the generous 0.25 litre size, which is more than a quarter of a bottle. All glasses carry gauge marks, but look around at the sizes of glasses on neighbouring tables to see what the measure may be! Wines from the 'open wine' selection, which is usually a wide range, may also be ordered by the 'Schoppen', when they are known as 'Schoppenweine'. This is an interesting term: the Schoppen was originally the measure of the contents of a glass and, today, the word implies a measure of a half litre. Open wines may be served by the carafe — Karaffenwein or Ausschankwein — will come in a measure as defined by local law, but it is usually a half litre (50 cl.).

Eating Places

A 'Ratskeller' is the cellar below the Town Hall (the Rathaus — 'Rat' is the Council) and is usually a good restaurant, where both wine and beer may be ordered. A 'Wirtschaft' is an establishment that is vaguely equivalent to the British term 'pub' — it will serve food as well as drinks and, occasionally, may even have rooms to let. The significance of the terms

'Restaurant' and 'Hotel' are evident, but it is worth bearing in mind that, in Germany, a 'Café' will serve hot and cold drinks, cakes and biscuits, light meals and wines and spirits. A 'Gasthaus' is an inn or a small hotel that also has a restaurant — which may be used by non-residents as well as those staying there. A 'Konditorei' is a type of tea-room or café, perhaps the Germany version of a French 'patisserie', usually associated with somewhere or someone making pastries, where you can order wine as well as tea, coffee or chocolate.

Something that travellers with families will certainly appreciate is the way in which children are not only allowed but welcome in licensed premises, so that inexpensive meals can be shared, as well as single dishes ordered for the very young. Bear in mind, though, that penalities in Germany for driving after drinking are very strict — if you are going out for an evening of wine, it is probably advisable to arrange for a driver.

Don't be put off from patronising a 'Bierkeller' or any restaurant that is associated with a brewery, as these too usually sell a good range of wines by the glass and bottle. Such places will also provide attractive, well-cooked food and so do even quite small cafés; you can go into a small, modestly-furnished place where you may only think it possible to get a drink, and find that they will be glad to serve informal food, such as omelettes, salads, scrambled eggs or a plate of assorted cold meats, cheese, sausages and pies. The 'cold table' at any good and certainly every luxury hotel can provide a wonderful selection of dishes at a reasonable price. But, of course, in such establishments no food can be expected to be really cheap.

In general, German food tends to be rather bland, mostly going well with the wines. Do not, however, expect the locals to order the finest wines, such as the great Auslesen, to be served with food in quite the same way as fine wines are served in other countries; such wines are reserved for leisurely appraisal outside the meal; sometimes a plain sponge or light fruit cake may be offered with them, or simply a few sweet biscuits. White bread is also somewhat traditional when serious tasting is being done — otherwise it is seldom seen.

Meals

Except in the bigger restaurants, you may order only one course if you wish — there may be a set menu, but it is perfectly in order to choose only one or two courses from it, for which you will be charged accordingly. There is nothing unusual or discourteous, either, about a group of people around a table ordering and eating different dishes, which they start on as each arrives, instead of waiting for a more formal progression of the meal and taking each course at a time.

Contrary to popular belief, the German does not eat sauerkraut every day — or even every month! There are also many dishes from other countries, such as Italian pasta, European specialities such as Serbian lentil soup with sausages (Yugoslavische Linsensuppe mit Wurst), and German versions of pies (Fleischpastete), smoked ham (geräuchte Schinken), plus, of course, sausages (Wurst) in enormous variety — it has been estimated that there are 1458 different types, but there may be many more — which are served both hot and cold.

Pasta (Makkaroni), noodles (Nudeln) and dumplings (Klösse) feature frequently on menus and dishes often come with a rich gravy.

Smoked eel (Räucheraal), which is very popular in the Mosel, herring (Hering) of all kinds, often served with onion or marinated and combined with onions, apples and sour cream (Hausfrauenart), smoked salmon (Räucherlachs) and smoked trout (Räucherforelle) are all first courses likely to be found in many eating places. Incidentally, with salads, which may feature as starters as well as main courses, the dressing will be made with little or no vinegar — and sometimes with milk — which means that even quite a delicate wine can be drunk without the acidity of the vinegar affecting it.

There is a definite north-south division of traditions in foods, marked by the 'Main Line' or River Main, which flows from east to west. To the north of this, vegetables of many different kinds will accompany meat and fish, but in southern Germany more filling accompaniments such as pasta and Spätzle, a type of ribbon pasta made of potato flour, act as 'padding'. Both cabbage (Kohl) and spinach (Spinat) are rarely served plain, but will be mashed up with cream or flavoured with herbs. Asparagus (Spargel) which in Germany is the white variety, is very good. It is served both hot, with melted butter, or cold with a type of vinaigrette.

Game is frequently included on menus, and venison (Wild) is very popular. It may be served in many different ways, usually with a thick gravy and sometimes the great culinary treat is saddle of venison (Rehrücken). Saddle of hare (Hasenrücken) is another speciality, often served with a type of blackberry sauce (Brombeere or Kronsbeere or Preiselbeere), or with apples or peas (Äpfel, Erbsen) and invariably with mushrooms (Pilz), notably the locally-grown ochre yellow type, pfifferling, which is a sort of chanterelle. Game birds are comparatively rare, except for partridge (Rebhuhn).

Liver (Leber), tongue in Madeira sauce with pease pudding (Zunge in Madeirasauce mit Erbsenbrei) or spinach, frankfurter-type sausages with lentils (Linsen mit Wurst) — a dish often served on a soup plate, as may be some of the soups with sausages in them — and beef marinated in wine then braised (Sauerbraten) are other dishes well worth trying.

Local specialities include saumagen, from Kallstadt — this is a stuffed sow's stomach, a Palatinate version of haggis, one might almost say — and the Pfalz onion soup (Pfälzer Zwiebelsuppe), which is also good to try. Visitors should be warned that, out in the country, appetites are often hearty and so portions may be very large, but it is often possible to ask for a small helping (kleine Portion) or else for one portion to be shared between two people (ein Portion für zwei), although this practice would be frowned on in the very best restaurants.

At Christmas, the traditional fare is goose (Gans), which like turkey (Truthahn) is served for many occasions all the year round. Goose cooked in the German way is non-greasy, with a delicious crisp skin. Chicken (Huhn) and duck (Ente) are widely available and so are many river fish, such as trout (Forelle), eel (Aal), pike (Hecht), carp (Karpfen) and tench (Schleie). Sea fish (Seefisch) are well cooked everywhere in Germany, especially turbot (Steinbutt) and halibut (Heilbutte), also sole (Seezunge). Near the coast you will find recommendations for shellfish (Schalenfisch) — by the way, a Schellfisch is a cod! There is no longer local salmon, which today is imported from Scotland or Norway.

Everyone in Germany tends to have a sweet tooth and, in addition to the usual ices, fruit salad and similar internationally-known sweet courses, there are quite often cold soufflés (Pudding) and elaborate pastries (Torte) which may be lavishly accompanied with whipped cream (Schlagsahne). The various fruit tarts, cakes and such seasonal delights as the Zwetschenkuchen, a type of plum tart that may be made in a round or square tin, should be sampled during the few weeks when it is made with the fresh fruit.

German cheeses are described later on, but the cheese board will often be provided with a variety of crispbread as well as rye and other breads, including several types of pumpernickel. Caraway seeds are sometimes in a little dish, forming part of the salt and pepper set on the table and many Germans use them as a seasoning, especially with cheese. There are also many different kinds of mustard (Senf) in Germany, ranging from the very mild to the extremely strong; you may be offered several sorts if you order a plate of cold meats or assorted sausages.

Of course, if you like everything very highly seasoned, you will probably opt for beer to drink instead of wine, but the open wines of the ordinary sort are possible too. Ideally, sample your wine before you eat anything very highly spiced that may change or overwhelm the flavour of the wine.

German hospitality can be lavish. However, be warned that even close friends may simply find it easier to entertain you in a restaurant rather than in their home — nowadays this is usual everywhere. Both lunch and dinner do tend to take place earlier than British visitors may expect — and they are served punctually, so that one should arrive on time. The German working day starts early, so, except on special occasions, people will have their evening meal early too. If you are asked to a wine and cheese party — this is a very popular form of entertaining — then this may take place at seven in the evening and be just that: wine and cheese. However, there will be plenty — and a variety — of both and all the refreshment will be as good as the host and hostess can make it.

If you are invited for a drink after dinner, you may as a special gesture be offered a bottle of something rare from the host's private cellar. This will be the sort of wine you are expected to sip and appraise. One bottle may lead to another — German wine lovers thoroughly enjoy sharing their treasures with other enthusiasts — so go slowly. Do not be surprised, either, if the very finest wines of all are served to you in rather smaller glasses than those used for the more ordinary wines; this is a tradition and an indication that the wine is intended to be discussed and drunk slowly for some time in a rather ceremonial fashion.

German bread

A huge range of different types of bread is made in Germany. About 200 different breads are exported; many more could be listed. There is a bread museum in a former hunting lodge at Mollenfelde, near Göttingen, where some of the exhibits date from four thousand years ago!

Visitors may find German breads a little strange, somewhat rough and heavy. The flour used is coarsely milled wholemeal, with rye making the dark breads and wheat the paler kinds.

Here are some of the main types of bread, for the traveller who may be buying food for a picnic or who would like to experiment when eating in catering establishments. They should all be cut very thin.

Kümmelbrot: Caraway seed bread, made of coarse wholemeal flour, medium brown in colour. This is often eaten with sausages and beer, or cheese and assorted cold cuts.
Landbrot: Farmhouse bread, made mainly of rye flour, in a flattish loaf that is round and has a grainy crust. The bread itself is a dark brown colour. This too is a traditional

accompaniment to sausages, cheese and caraway and beer.

Grahambrot: This coarse-grained wheat bread is named after the US Dr Sylvester Graham. It is a wholemeal bread that has had the bran content separated by a special process. The carbohydrate content is low.

Pumpernickel: This is perhaps the best known of all German breads. It is a coarse rye wholemeal, deep brown and, on account of its assertive flavour, it is presented in thin slivers; pumpernickel for export comes in squares, oblongs or rounds, but, in Germany, bakers make it in many different shapes. A little goes a long way — it is widely used as a base for cheese.

'Toast' is made of light-coloured bread, in the international way. Crispbreads of many kinds are also widely available. Otherwise, German breads are generally more substantial than the breads of many western countries and the visitor will find that, because of this, a smaller amount will be enough for them. To most people, visitor and resident alike, the most welcome form of German bread is the basket of fresh rolls (Brötchen) which appears daily on every breakfast table.

Sauerkraut

The ancient Egyptians knew how to make a version of sauerkraut and; because it probably was first evolved in the East, their 'know how' spread to Rome. After the Dark Ages, the Tartars brought sauerkraut recipes with them to Europe. This economical dish, a form of pickled cabbage, was known to the great ecclesiastical houses of Europe and definitely in Germany, where the cabbage seems to have been grown since early times. It may have often been the only winter green vegetable available there and its bulk would have provided a satisfying dish as well as one that (although this would not have been recognised) gave the consumers valuable vitamins into the bargain.

The base of the dish is white cabbage, the type that has a long core or stem. This cabbage is first shredded and then put into what, in former times, would have been a wooden cask or keg — possibly even an old wine cask. In between each layer, salt, of the coarse type, is sprinkled and, when the container is full, a cover is put on the cabbage mixture, though this must be one that allows air to get to the vegetable, even while keeping it firmly pressed down. The cabbage then begins to ferment — it becomes 'sour'. With the arrival of tinned and frozen vegetables, available all the year round, sauerkraut has declined in both importance and popularity. Nevertheless, although hopeless with wine, it is a substantial and economical dish, and thus one worth knowing about. A luxury sauerkraut 'garni' may include several sorts of smoked meat, together with several different types of sausage, with, possibly, the addition of wine and potatoes. A simpler version may merely be a sausage or two on top of the cabbage. But, even if the consumer of sauerkraut arrives at the reasonable conclusion that beer is probably the best drink with this dish, no traveller in Germany should miss trying the recipe at least once — for, when it is the product of a kitchen rather than a tin, sauerkraut can be very enjoyable.

Cheeses

Vast quantities of cheese are made in Germany, from the hard matured variety to the soft, fresh curd type. It would require a separate book to list even the principal cheeses but, as the visitor will note, the cheese board is everywhere very much in demand, and wine and cheese parties are very popular, so the following brief list may help in selection. It should also be remembered that the finer wines tend to be too delicate for drinking with assertively-flavoured cheeses; the Germans will partner cheese with wines of everyday quality or, perhaps even better, with beer.

Allgäu Emmental, a cow's milk cheese in classic style, made in the Bavarian mountains on the border with Austria, is a firmish cheese, with rounded holes in it.

The term 'Schnittkäse' means 'sliceable cheese' and is used to differentiate cheeses that are either really hard, like **Tilsit** (pale yellow with tiny holes), or semi-hard, such as **Weisslackerkäse** (sharp, with definite 'bite'), **Wilstermarschkäse,** also with holes, a slightly sour taste and a touch of herby flavour, **Edelpilzkäse,** the outstanding example of blue cheese to be made in Germany, and **Steinbuscherkäse,** straw-coloured and somewhat buttery in style. **Romadurkäse,** with a brownish-red skin and a few holes in it, spicy **Limburger,** and wine cheese **(Weinkäse),** which is made in small rounds and is mild in flavour, are other softish cheeses.

The fresh cheeses are available in great variety: they sometimes have chopped onions, chives or other flavourings mixed into them. **Quark** is curd cheese, **Schichtkäse** ('layer cheese') is made from layers of skimmed milk curd and full fat curd — it can easily be identified because these layers show in white or yellowish stripes when it is cut.

From Mainz and the Harz Mountains come many sour curd cheeses, yellowish to reddish-brown in colour, strong when fresh and becoming very pungent as they mature. The term 'Handkäse' (hand cheese) is often used when referring to them because, originally, they were shaped by hand, rather than in moulds.

In addition to these native cheeses, German cheese producers also make types of the other classic cheeses, such as the Dutch-, French- and Italian-style cheeses, which will be featured under their well-known names.

Appendices

1

Wine Tasting

by Pamela Vandyke Price

There is nothing difficult about tasting wine, even if some people suppose it to be a mystery requiring a long initiation process! The aim of tasting is to discover an enjoyable wine, either enjoyable to drink immediately or likely to prove enjoyable after some period of maturation.

Wine is a beautiful and interesting commodity — and those who really know something about it and care for it are delighted to share their enjoyment and appreciation with even the humblest beginner as well as with the experienced. So do not be shy of trying to taste seriously. Ask questions and whenever possible try to note down your impressions of a wine *while* you are tasting it — even an hour later, your thoughts will lack precison. Also, if you remember in detail wines that you like or do not like your future shopping for wine is greatly helped. No-one wants to risk being a wine bore or wine snob, but the world of wine lovers is worthy of exploration.

First Look at the Wine's Appearance

A tasting sample will only occupy a small space in the glass. Its appearance has much to reveal. Ideally, the glass should be perfectly clear and clean and on a stem, though in some regions you may have to make do with small tumblers or possibly a tasting cup of special type.

The wine should be clear and bright, with something 'living' about it. Do not be concerned that there may be bits (known as 'flyers') in it, as these may be particles from a cask sample, which subsequent filtration may well remove. Their presence, very often, indicates a quality wine, and therefore they are not reasons for condemning the wine in any way.

Tilt the glass away from you at approximately an angle of 45° and hold it against something white, so that you can examine the colour. The living quality should be obvious, rather in the way that the water of a spring is different from the flat dull water drawn from a tap and left to stand for several days. Whether the wine is red or white, it should be pleasant, ideally beautiful to look at and give pleasure to the eye.

Smell the Wine

A wine should have a pleasant healthy smell, which, in certain wines, can be complex but which should always give enjoyment. You will realise this and be able to sniff it more easily if you circulate the wine in the glass, holding the glass by the stem or, possibly, by the foot (not as difficult as it looks at the outset) and simply swinging the liquid round, putting your nose into the glass at intervals and sniffing. The aeration of the wine releases the fragrance.

Surprisingly, very few wines actually 'smell of the grape' although people often wish that they might! A few grapes, notably the Muscat, do possess a distinctive aroma, which is quite often easily identified as 'grapiness', but otherwise although certain grapes may result in wines smelling of those grapes, the associations with fruit are not always obvious. A wine should smell fresh and clean, but there are certain smells which, with young wines, may be present for a short time, indicating nothing more than that the wine is going through a phase of natural development.

These smells include the slightly beery smell which may mean the wine is still undergoing a stage of fermentation, a vaguely yeasty smell, which sometimes seems present when a wine has recently been bottled, a slightly sharp smell, often described as 'green', which may be present in even the best made wine in a year when the grapes have been unable to ripen perfectly. Or, in some instances, this green smell may mean that the vineyard contains a high proportion of young vines, the use of which is apparent in the early stages of the wine's development. Obviously woody smells can mean that the wine has been matured in new wood, this smell passing with time also, or, if the woodiness is of a soggy sort, it may mean that there is a faulty stave in the cask in which the wine has been matured.

You are unlikely to find 'corked' wine in a sample of a very young, bottled wine, but a complete absence of smell can be slightly sinister in this respect, indicating that something is preventing the wine from giving off its fragrance. It is the 'swimming bath' smell, reminiscent of chlorine, that is for me most definitely assoicated with corkiness — which, by the way, has nothing whatsoever to do with bits of cork being in the wine. Some people do find that corkiness reminds them of the smell of cork, but I have never been able to see this myself. A musty smell can be indicative of an ill-made wine, but it should not be confused with 'bottle stink'. This is the smell (that is often stale and flat) of the little quantity of air held in the bottle of wine under the cork, which may affect the taste of the first portion poured. A little aeration will cause this to pass very soon.

The good smells, interesting and pleasing to the nose, include a type of fruitiness, the different sorts of which will be associated with the various types of grape when the taster has gained a little experience. Young wines, especially those that are most enjoyable when drunk fairly young when they are at their peak of freshness, usually have an obvious fruity smell. Then there is a crisp almost sharp smell, like the freshness of a good apple, which can indicate the right kind of acidity balancing the fruit. This should be noticed in most young wines, especially those that are dry and light. Wines from cool vineyards tend to have more smell than wines from hot ones. The infinity of delicate, flowery, herby, and subtle depths of scent with which some of the great German and other northern vineyards are associated, and in the reds from vineyards where the vine has to struggle, such as Burgundy and Bordeaux, can be so beautiful, even while the wines are very young that, as is sometimes said, 'it is almost unnecessary to drink when the smell is so fascinating'.

With the finest wines, try to break up the general impression made on you by the smell into the first impact, anything that then reveals itself by further aeration, and finally see whether there appears to be some subtle, as yet unrevealed fragrance underneath the other smell. Wines are like people in this respect, the more obvious are not always the most rewarding. Sometimes, right at the end of a tasting, a smell can come out of a wine glass that may indicate something to look forward to in the future. Try to remain alert to register this if it is there.

Taste the Wine

Always adapt tasting techniques to what experience has taught you suits your own abilities best. But the most usual way to taste is to draw a very small quantity of wine — about a teaspoonful — into the mouth, accompanied by a small amount of air. There is no need to make a loud sucking noise while doing this, but the circumstance of pulling the wine into the mouth, plus some air, seems to sharpen up the impression it can make. Then circulate the wine in your mouth, pulling it over the tongue, letting it run along the sides of the mouth and getting a general 'feel' of what it is like: light/dry/sweetish/thick/thin/assertive/reticent/chewy/attaching itself to the sides of the mouth/attacking the gums (everyone's gums tend to ache after a lot of tasting!) Try to split up the numerous impressions which the wine may have to give you before you spit it out. Don't be hesitant about taking another sample if necessary.

AFTER-TASTE AND FINISH

When you have tasted the wine and have spat out the sample, breathe out sharply — you will be aware of an extra smell, rather than a taste, that passes across the palate. This is the after-taste and it can reveal quite a lot about the wine: for example, it may be far more definitely fragrant than the original bouquet or smell, or it may have a lingering quality, known in wine terms as 'length', both of which can indicate that the wine has great promise and may develop considerably. Or there can be little or no after-taste, when a wine may be described as 'short'.

The way in which the wine leaves the palate is the 'finish'. Does it finish cleanly, or has it a trace of stickiness? Has it a final flourish of flavour, a definite extra touch of taste, or does it die away rapidly? The finish of any good wine, regardless of price, should be clean, and, with a fine wine, entice the drinker to take more. With a modest type of wine, the finish should at least refresh rather than cloy the palate.

Tasting in Germany

Visitors who have previously gained their experience of tasting wine in other countries may find it strange to adopt the German practice, whereby it is quite usual — apart from purely professional tastings — to be expected to taste while you are sitting down, from a sample in a small, tumbler-like glass — and frequently without the option of spitting, either on to the floor or into a sink or spittoon! Of course, most German wines are drinkable, albeit not at their peak, at least as soon as they are bottled, so that they are palatable at a youthful stage, compared with many other wines, especially red wines from other wine countries.

When you are tasting, it is always advisable to spit the wines out; otherwise you will saturate your palate and lose the ability to make fine differentiations. With the very finest sweet wines, however, it would be discourteous to spit out a sample of something that will eventually be part of a costly bottle so, as this kind of wine may usually be offered as a treat and at the end of a visit, there is every incentive to drink it; otherwise, samples poured may be carefully returned to the cask.

The British are apparently the only people who prefer to taste while standing up. Can German influence be at least partly responsible for the way many tastings in the US take place with the participants seated? Of course, the visitor who wants to stand up to taste will seldom find it impossible to do so, though he may be a little conspicuous.

2

Glossary of Wine Terms

The following are words or expressions most likely to be found or heard in relation to wine, which are not always in dictionaries, or if they are, may not be used in the same way as they are in relation to wine.

It should be noted that, in Germany, nouns have capital letters but verbs do not. This is why the verbs here, even when they come at the beginning of a line, do not have capital letters.

Die Anbaugebiete — **The wine regions**
Das (bestimmte) Anbaugebiet — (Specified) wine-growing region
Der Bereich — Wine district
Die Gemeinde — Parish, wine-growing community
Die Lage, Die Weinbergslage — Wine-growing site, vineyard site (as entered in the vineyard register)
Die Einsellage — Vineyard within defined boundaries
Die Grosslage — Group of Einzellagen with similar characteristics

Im Weinberg — **In the vineyard**
Der Wingert (colloquial) — Vineyard
Das Weingut — Wine estate, single property
Der Verwalter — Administrator
Der Winzer — Wine grower
Die Weintraube, die Weinbeere — Grape, the actual fruit
Der Weinstock, der Rebstock — Vine stock, vine (i.e. the plant itself)
Die Rebsorte — The particular variety of vine
Der Pfahl, der Weinbergspfahl — Stake for vine, pole
Der Weinbergsdraht — Wire for training
Die Blüte, die Rebenblüte — Flowering (of the vine)
Die Weinbergblüte — The flowering (of the vine)
Die Weinlese, die Herbstlese — The picking, gathering of grapes, harvest

Die Edelfäule — Noble rot, botrytis cinerea
Der Winkel, der Neigungswinkel — Angle (of the vineyard), the slope
Die Lage (Südlage, Nordlage) — Aspect or outlook (southern, northern)

Das Aufziehen mit Draht und Weinbergspfählen — Training with wire and props or poles
Das Aufziehen nur mit Pfählen — Training with poles only
hoch — high
breit — broad (horizontal)
Der Abstand von Rebstock zu Rebstock — The distance between the individual vines (significant because of the amount of air they get)

Der Abstand zwischen Reihen	The distance between rows (significant because of mechanical or manual cultivation)
Der Rebschnitt, das Schneiden	(The method of) pruning
Das Zurückschneiden auf zwei Augen	Pruning back to two buds (the most usual method for quality wines)
propfen, aufpropfen, veredeln okulieren	To graft

Der Boden, die Erde — **Soil**

Der Sand	Sand
Der Schiefer	Slate, Schist
(Das Rheinisches Schiefergebirge	The Rhineland Schist Massif)
Der Kies	Gravel
Der Ton, der Lehm	Clay
Der Löss	Loess
Der Kalk, der Kalkstein	Limestone
Der Granit	Granite

Im Keller — **In the cellar**

Die Maische	The must or unfermented grape juice (still with skins in it)
Der Most	The must (with the skins removed)
Das Holzfass	A cask (wooden)
Das Doppelstuck	2400 litre cask
Das Stuck	1200 litre cask
Das Halbstück	600 litre cask
Das Viertelstück	300 litre cask
Das Fuder	960-1000 litre cask (term particular to the Mosel and Pfalz)
Der Filter	A filter
filtrieren	To filter
schönen	To fine
Die Kelter	Wine press (in general)
Die Weinbereitung, der Weinausbau ⎫ Die Kellerwirtschaft ⎭	Vinification
Der Ausbau in Holzfässern	Vinification in separate wooden casks — i.e. cask by cask
Ein Grosses Fass, ein Behälter, ein Tank	A vat
Das Verschnittfass, der Verschnittank, Der Verschnittbehälter	The blending cask, or the vat
verschneiden	To blend
vergären	To ferment
Das Gärfass, der Gärtank	A fermentation cask or a vat
Wein ausbauen, reifen	To mature
Verbessern, anreichern	To sweeten the must with sugar
abfüllen	To bottle
Die Flaschenfüllung, die Abfüllung auf Flaschen	The process of bottling
Die Rheinflasche	Rhine wine bottle (amber)
Die Moselflasche	Mosel wine bottle (blue-green)
Der Bocksbeutel	The dumpy flagon of Franconia
Die Burgunderflasche	Burgundy bottle (dumpy, with sloping shoulders)
Die Bordeauxflasche	Bordeaux bottle (square-shouldered bottle)

Die Literflasche	Litre bottle
Die halbe Flasche	Half bottle
Die Viertelflasche	Quarter bottle
Das Etikett	The label
Das Rumpfetikett	The body or main label
Die Fuss-Schleife	A strip label, below the main label
Die Halsschleife	The neck label
Die Amtliche Prüfungsnummer (AP)	Official control number (test number)
Der Tafelwein	(A blend of EEC) table wine
Der Deutsche Tafelwein	German table wine
Qualitätswein bestimmter Anbaugebiete (QbA)	Quality wine of a specific region (of the eleven)
Qualitätswein mit Prädikat	Quality wine with a special attribute
Kabinett	Above average
Die Spätlese	Late selection; made from late harvested grapes
Die Auslese	Special selection; made from specially selected bunches of grapes
Die Beerenauslese	Special selection of single berries; made from late harvested and selected individual grapes
Die Trockenbeerenauslese	Made from late harvested, individually selected grapes dried on the vine
Der Eiswein	Wine made from grapes with their water content frozen by frost
Die Winzergenossenschaft	Wine-growers' co-operative
Die Erzeugerabfüllung	Bottled by the producer
Die Kapsel	The capsule
Der Korken	The cork
Der Korkenzieher	A corkscrew

Die Weinprobe	**Wine tasting**
schlecht; gut	Bad; good
klein; gross	Small and small-scale; big, fine
Die Klarheit, die Helligkeit	Brightness, clarity
hell	Clear, bright
bauernhell	Falling bright after fermentation, but without filtering
glanzhell	Crystal clear, star bright
blind	Cloudy
trüb	Very cloudy — not bright
Der Schleier	Haze
Die Farbe	Colour
leicht	Light, pale in colour
grün	Green
gelb	Yellow
goldgelb	Golden
dunkles Gold	Dark gold, amber
bernsteinfarbig	Amber
hochfarbig	Deep amber — i.e. browning
Das Bukett	Bouquet or smell
leicht	Light

voll	Full
zart	Delicate
duftig	Fragrant
blumig	Flowery
fruchtig	Fruity, full
würzig	Spicy, aromatic (e.g. Gewürztraminer — the spicy Traminer)
aufdringlich	Obtrusive, obvious
stark	Full, strong, assertive
Der Geschmack	The taste
Die Blume	The flavour
Ein leichter Wein	A light wine (i.e. one low in alcohol or texture)
Ein schwerer Wein	A wine high in alcohol — or heavy and full of essence
spritzig	Pétillant, prickly, very slightly sparkling
nicht spritzig	Still
kurz	Short
kräftig	Powerful
vollmundig	Rounded, full-bodied
die Fülle	Luscious style, fullness
reif	Mature
firn	Over the top, past its peak, with some oxidation
harmonisch	Balanced
rassig	Breed — a wine displaying its fine pedigree
durchgegoren	Very dry
Die Süsse	Sweetness
nachhaltig	Lingering, a wine that lasts on the palate
fruchtig	Fruity
charmant	Charming
bezauberend, faszinierend	Fascinating
Der Nachgeschmack	The after-taste
Das Probierglas	A tasting glass (usually a small, tumbler-type glass)
Das Stengelglas	A tasting glass with a stem
Der Spucknapf, der Spuckkasten	A spittoon
ausspucken	To spit
proben, probieren, verkosten	To taste
Die Probe, die Weinprobe	A sample, a taste, a tasting
eingiessen, ausgiessen, einschenken	To pour
Ein Wein zum Aufheben	A wine to keep (i.e. it will get better)
Ein Wein zum Hinlegen	A wine to put away (i.e. a wine to reserve — to lay down)
Ein süffiger Wein	A wine that's easy to drink — very pleasing
schlürfen	To roll around one's palate, i.e. to slurp back
schlucken	To swallow

3

Further Reading

There are numerous books written about German wines, but, for the purposes of this list, only those that have been translated into English are given here. In libraries it is possible to refer to many that provide interesting background to the whole subject, but caution is advised if these are very out of date — the whole picture has changed radically in recent years. Such books can, of course, be handy for looking up historical matters. It is also worth bearing in mind that the opinions of authors can vary greatly as regards such a personal matter as wine; sometimes a writer will feel strongly about one aspect of his subject and give the impression that what he states is fact — whereas much if not all may really be his personal opinion. This is why I would advise the serious student of German wines to read widely on the subject, without, at the outset, regarding every single book as gospel, however much it may appeal to the individual. The books that I suggest in this short list, however, are all generally reliable although, as with any book about wine, some or all of them may be out of date by the time you are reading this text, as far as regulations and technicalities are concerned.

Maps

An excellent touring map for the driver and as regards general orientation is the Michelin 987 (1:1,000,000). This covers the whole of Germany as well as neighbouring countries, so includes the towns of Amsterdam, Brussels, Paris, Berne, Vienna, Prague, the East German Republic and the southern part of Denmark. Maps showing the region in more detail and equally good are the Michelin 202, 203, 204, 205 and 206 (1:200,000); these cover all the wine areas except for Franconia.

Other good maps are the series German General map (Deutsche Generalkark 1:200,000), issued in co-operation with Shell, and the Aral map (1:400,000), which is published by Kartographischer Verlag Busche GmbH, Dortmund. RV Traveller and Traffic (RV Reise-und Verkehrsverlag, Stuttgart) have a useful map (1:200,000) of the Wiesbaden/Wurzburg line southwards and another of the

Rhineland, and Fietz Verlag Frankfurt have a special map of 90 kilometres around Frankfurt (1:150,000), which includes most of the important areas, with the exception of part of Franconia and the Mosel Valley.

Maps specially for hikers are usually most easily obtained locally; they are generally reliable and well designed.

Books

The Red Michelin *Germany* is most useful to the motorist, as it gives in four languages all the essential information on hotels, restaurants, towns and villages, with distances and detailed maps of towns.

The Green Michelin *Guide to Germany* is published in an English edition and is probably the most concise, intelligent and best written guide. It provides excellent historical and geographical details and has a well thought out scheme whereby places and individual sights are graded from the tourist angle.

Of all wine books, the most useful for the traveller's pocket is Hans Ambrosi's *Wine Atlas Germany and Dictionary,* published in English by the Ceres-Verlag Rudolf-August Oekter KG, Bielefeld. It contains an up-to-date atlas, complete with place and vineyard index and allows the tourist to pinpoint the geographical situation of any vineyard he wishes to visit. The dictionary in English under German headings is the most useful source of easily obtainable information on all matters for the traveller. Also by Hans Ambrosi and now in English, is *Where the Great German Wines Grow* (published by Hastings House, New York). This gives excellent thumb-nail sketches of some ninety of the finest wine estates. The information is intelligently presented, giving approach roads, position, size, vine species, general impact and impression. The book is perhaps somewhat more technical than the average tourist may be prepared to take and few of the estates which the author describes are prepared to receive visitors from outside the trade, but it is an essential for the serious student.

The *German Wine Atlas* (published in English for the Stabilisation Fund in Mainz and by Davis-Poynter in London) contains the same atlas and index as Dr Ambrosi's; it is larger in format and also contains much sound information for the tourist and wine lover on what to see as well as detailed descriptions and pictures of each region, but lacks the dictionary.

Hans Meinhard's *German Wines,* originally published by Oriel, has recently been re-issued as *Wines of Germany* (David & Charles). It is a pleasant book and gives a considerable amount of detail, although it is occasionally rather heavy going. Walter Marsden's *The Rhineland* (Batsford) is a descriptive travel book, taking the tourist through the Rhineland from north of Koblenz, along the Mosel and right down to Heidelberg, although it excludes the regions to the south and east of this. The author deals pleasantly with local lore and history, although the actual wine information is slight.

Among books published some time ago, prior to the full impact of the 1971 German Wine Law, there are several that should certainly be consulted. O. W. Loeb and Terence Prittie's *Moselle* (Faber) and Alfred Langenbach's *German Wines and Vines* (Vista) are both excellent. There are also several good reference books in English published in the UK and US, including Alexis Lichine's *Encyclopedia of Wines and Spirits* (Cassell) and *German Wines* by S. F. Hallgarten (Faber). These may be found in reference libraries, although the layman may find them rather too technical, with much statistical and similar information that can be rather deterring. The tourist will, of course, be able to find souvenir booklets, lavishly illustrated, in all the main wine regions and there are generally captions and some part of the text of these given in English, should an English language edition not be available.

4

Useful Addresses

The following are the headquarters of organisations that will provide information about German wines:

General

Deutsches Weininstitut GmbH, Gutenbergplatz 3-5, 6500 Mainz.

German Regional Centres

Ahr: Gebietsweinwerbung Ahr e.V., Elligstrasse 14, 5483 Bad Neuenahr-Ahrweiler.
Baden: Weinwerbezentrale Badischer Winzergenossenschaften, Ettlinger Strasse 12, 7500 Karlsruhe 1.
Franken: Frankenwein-Frankenland e.V., Postfach 764, 8700 Würzburg 2.
Hessische Bergstrasse: Weinbauverband Hessische Bergstrasse e.V., Konigsberger Strasse 4, 6148 Heppenheim/Bergstrasse.
Mittelrhein: Mittelrhein-Burgen und Weine/e.V., Rathausstrasse 8, 5423 Braubach.
Mosel-Saar-Ruwer: Weinwerbung Mosel-Saar-Ruwer e.V., Neustrasse 86, 5500 Trier.
Nahe: Weinland Nahe e.V., Am Kornmarkt 6, 6550 Bad Kreuznach.
Rheingau: Der Rheingau-Der Weingau, Weinwerbung e.V., Im alten Rathaus, 6225 Johannisberg, Rheingau.
Rheinhessen: Rheinhessenweine e.V., 117er Ehrenhof 5, 6500 Mainz.
Rheinpfalz: Rheinpfalz-Weinpfalz e.V., Friedrich-Ebert-Strasse 11-13, 6730 Neustadt a.d.W.
Württemberg: Werbegemeinschaft Württembergischer Weingärtnergenossenschaft, Heilbronner Strasse 41, 7000 Stuttgart 1.

Information services in other countries

Canada: German Wine Information Service, 20 Eglinton Avenue E., Toronto, Ontario, M4P 1A9.
Denmark: Informationsservice for Tyske Vine, Landemaerket 51, 1119 Kobenhavn K.
England: Wines from Germany Information Service, 121

Gloucester Place, London W.1.
Japan: Japan-Public-Relations, Inc., 767 Othemachi Building, 1-6-1 Othemachi-Ku, Tokyo 100.
Netherlands: Informatiebureau voor Duitse Wijn, Wibautstraat 12, Amsterdam.
Sweden: Tysk Vin Information, Roslagsgatan 56, 11354 Stockholm.
USA: German Wine Information Bureau, Sixth Floor, 666 Fifth Avenue, New York, NY 10019.

Colleges and research stations concerned with viticulture

For the really serious student, this list may be of use, although it should be emphasized that these establishments are primarily concerned with work for the wine trade and cannot receive visitors unless an appointment has been made. Usually, someone can deal with correspondence in English but of course the visitor planning any programme at this level ought to be able to speak some German.

The institute at Geisenheim is particularly famous, and its work contributes to the study and making of wine throughout the world. It is Geisenheim that has advised the English Vineyards Association and many of its members and the Director, Dr Karl Becker, is a respected and popular personality known throughout the whole world of wine.

The most important colleges, all organised and controlled by the relevant 'Land' government, are the following:

Training College and Research Station for Agriculture, Viticulture and Horticulture at Maximilianstrasse 43, 6730 Neustadt. (Landes- Lehr- u. Forschungsanstalt für Landwirtschaft, Weinbau und Gartenbau) — Palatinate.
Training College and Research Station for Viticulture and Horticulture in 6222 Geisenheim. (Lehr- und Forschungsanstalt für Wein- und Gartenbau) — Rheingau.
Training College and Research and Experimental Station in 6555 Bad Kreuznach. (Lehr- und Versuchsanstalt für Weinbau und Gartenbau) — Nahe.
Training College and Research and Experimental Station in 6504 Oppenheim. (Lehr- und Versuchsanstalt für Weinbau und Gartenbau) — Rheinhessen.
Training College and Research and Experimental Station in 5500 Trier. (Lehr- und Versuchsanstalt für Weinbau und Gartenbau) — Mosel.
Training College and Research and Experimental Station in 5482 Ahrweiler. (Lehr- und Versuchsanstalt für Weinbau und Gartenbau) — Ahr.
Bavarian State Training and Research Station in 8700

Wurzburg. (Bayerische Landesanstalt) — Franconia.
State Training College for Viticulture in 7102 Weinsberg.
(Staatliche Lehranstalt für Weinbau und Gartenbau) —
Württemberg.
Research Station for Viticulture in 7800 Freiburg.
(Weinbau-Institut, Merzhauserstrasse 119) — Baden.

Index